ORGANIZATIONAL RESPONSE TO CHANGING COMMUNITY SYSTEMS

ORGANIZATIONAL RESPONSE TO CHANGING COMMUNITY SYSTEMS

David F. Gillespie, *University of Washington*
Dennis S. Mileti, *Colorado State University*
Ronald W. Perry, *University of Hartford*

The Comparative Administration Research Institute
Graduate School of Business Administration
Kent State University

COLLEGE OF BUSINESS ADMINISTRATION
GRADUATE SCHOOL OF BUSINESS ADMINISTRATION
Gail E. Mullin, *Dean*

COMPARATIVE ADMINISTRATION RESEARCH INSTITUTE
Anant R. Negandhi, *Director*

This volume is published in collaboration with The Socio-Economic & Political Consequences of Earthquake Prediction, Department of Sociology, Colorado State University

ISBN: 0-87338-196-3
Library of Congress Catalog Card Number: 76-25890
Distributed by The Kent State University Press

Gillespie, David F
Organizational response to changing community systems.
Bibliography: p.
1. Neighbors in Need (Organization) 2. Organizational change—Case studies. 3. Seattle—Economic conditions. I. Mileti, Dennis S., joint author. II. Perry. Ronald W., joint author. III. Title.
HV99.S732N45 301.36′3 76-25890
ISBN 0-87338-196-3

In Memory of
FRANCES E. GILLESPIE

Contents

FIGURES

ACKNOWLEDGMENTS

The acquisition of case study data, especially of the longitudinal type, is particularly demanding of the persons in the organization under study. In this instance, the participating members of *Neighbors in Need* (NIN) not only gave of their time, effort and information, but they also willingly provided ready access to records and reports generated as part of NIN's operations. We wish to express our appreciation to the members of NIN with special thanks to Steve R. Williams and the NIN research staff.

We want to convey our gratitude to Ed Gross, J. Eugene Haas, and Rod Stark, who have been instrumental in stimulating and cultivating our interests in the area of complex organizations. It will be clear to their students the degree to which their influence has shaped the way we have viewed this organization.

A number of persons have served as insightful critics for various portions of this book as it was being developed. They helped us push our ideas further and express them with greater clarity. Critical comments and suggestions were offered by Roy Lotz, Bill Anderson, David Whetten, Ray Adamek, Dick Koenig, and Anant Negandhi.

Some of the material used in this writing was obtained from the library of the Disaster Research Center, The Ohio State University. We are grateful to DRC for opening its doors and allowing us permission to use such material. However, the Disaster Research Center is in no way responsible for the way the materials have been used, the interpretations made, or the analyses undertaken.

The financial support for this study came from three sources. First, our effort was partially supported by the National

Science Foundation—RANN (contract number HEW 74-24079) which is gratefully acknowledged. Second, support by the Office of Child Development—HEW (contract number 90-C-430) which is being conducted within the Center for Social Welfare Research, School of Social Work, University of Washington is also gratefully acknowledged. Finally, our sincere appreciation is due to the Comparative Administration Research Institute, Kent State University, which is primarily responsible for publishing this study. The opinions, findings, conclusions and recommendations expressed in this book, however, are those of the authors and do not necessarily reflect the views of the supporting organizations.

During the evolution of this book, two persons have, with undeviating cheerfulness,transformed our scribbles to legible typewritten pages and retyped several versions. We owe grateful acknowledgment to Elaine Sundt and Sandy Brown for their careful and skillful efforts in making the manuscripts as technically correct as possible. We are indebted as well to the additional services provided by the secretarial staffs in the Department of Sociology at Colorado State University, and the Center for Social Welfare Research at the University of Washington.

Finally we wish to express unfeigned gratitude to our families for contributing the kind of support that makes life worth living. Their willingness to avoid encroachment on time that rightfully belonged to them, and still keep smiling, is unexplainable, but it clearly made possible what otherwise would have been impossible. In particular, Irene Gillespie and Paula Perry have contributed immeasurably to the production of this book.

Preface

This book reports upon the emergence and development of *Neighbors in Need* (NIN), a Seattle, Washington based welfare organization. The purpose of this study is to develop a model facilitating the prediction of organizational persistence or dissolution. The birth processes of the organization described here are not essentially different from those of other groups and organizations. We have all seen organizations come to life when some individual or group has perceived, defined and communicated a sense of need to the community. Typically, however, such organizations dissolve within a relatively short period of time. But NIN's career pattern shows a persistence beyond the period of perceived need. Because of the long-term progressive nature of the community's stress, we were afforded the rare opportunity to use the case study method in an analytic rather than descriptive mode. Our purpose here, therefore, is to detail the analytic use of case study materials, thereby revealing our procedures to our colleagues and informing our students.

In general, analytic studies can be distinguished from descriptive studies in that they are framed in a design of logical proof (cf. Cohen and Nagel, 1934:249-272). They demand that the research design be constructed in such a way that logic will dictate the acceptance or rejection of one's hypothesis on the basis of the data collected. The factors attending the production of an analytic study, as Selltiz et al. (1959:83-88) and many others have noted, focus for the most part on the issues of generalization, correlation, spuriousness, and time-order. As would be expected, different study designs vary in their ability to illustrate time-order relationships, and to rule out sample bias, chance correlation, or spuriousness. To these ends, there is no question that experiments and multivariate analyses provide the most rigorous means for dealing with these issues; however, this in no way vitiates the usefulness of designing a case study along analytic lines. Many examples exist. Price (1960:127-219) illustrates how longitudinal case studies, by examining the same unit of analysis over time, provide sufficient evidence for inferring time-order relationships and for discounting spuriousness. In other words, longitudinal case studies provide the means whereby two out of the four criteria characterizing analytic studies can be met. However, with a sample of one, it is impossible to illustrate correlation between the concepts in our study. It is also beyond the limits of our study to generalize. However, through the stating of our assumptions and the generation of a general model, which was substantiated by our case, we switched the focus from a descriptive mode to an analytic one (cf. Whetten, 1975).

We may now ask, how can prediction be enhanced by the utilization of the case study technique to corroborate hypotheses? By definition, hypotheses predict (Cohen and Nagel, 1934:201). To the extent that a hypothesis or set of hypotheses are not invalidated, prediction appears to have been facilitated. It is true, however, that we can not put much more than little credence in our ability to generalize with an *N* of one; nevertheless, one is better than none. In addition, the use of certain elements or events as indicators for abstract concepts enables the findings of other researchers using the same concepts to be admissible as evidence. In this light, we used the specific details connected with NIN's emergence and development as a basis from which to infer general concepts. Specifically, our findings indicated that "environmental change," "community demands for service," "organizational capacity," "formalization," and "task orientations" were key factors in predicting the emergence and persistence of organizations in collective stress situations. Brought together into a causal model, it is possible to predict organizational emergence, persistence or demise. By using abstract concepts, the empirical findings from varied case studies can be drawn upon to validate or invalidate a particular hypothesis or set of hypotheses. In the event that a variety of different case studies fail to invalidate a given model, we propose that prediction has been facilitated.

Finally, how was our model constructed? To develop a model first and then test it with a single case would, as a rule, yield little compensation for the time, effort and expense required to gather case study data. In the opposite light, had we waited until all the data were in hand and then arranged it into an explanatory schema, we would have contributed only conjecture. Our model was actually constructed by a process somewhere between these polar extremes. The collection of our data and the construction of our model were actually inextricably intertwined. Blau and Meyer (1971: 85-86) note that "case study methods do not require the investigator to specify detailed hypotheses in advance. He may have a tentative list of propositions he wishes to test, but these can be modified and reformulated in the course of the research. Conclusions are reached by observing sequences of events and imputing a causal nexus to them." Stated differently, neither *a priori* intuition nor *post hoc* assemblage provided the means by which we achieved our model. Perhaps the process of retroduction (Schrag, 1967) best describes our analytic use of case study materials.

Initiating our efforts with the descriptive accounts in the disaster literature and the general scheme suggested by Emery and Trist (1965, 1972) we attempted to specify, through the technique of making successive approximations between theoretical concepts and the relevant evidence (Schrag, 1967: 237), the organizational processes attending emergence and development. Heretofore, the only analytic efforts in this body of literature were those found in the area of collective behavior (cf. Perry et al., 1974: 112f). These models are, however, entirely social-psychological in nature (Lotz and Gillespie, 1973: 14-15). We were interested in understanding the causal nexus characterizing organizational emergence and development in structural terms.

Those who have been trained in the virtues of large-scale comparative research may be unaware, as Blau and Meyer (1971: 87) point out, "that case studies have several advantages over the comparative method. Case studies provide intensive information in depth about social processes; they permit greater flexibility in the choice of variables to be studied; they allow the researcher to generate and test new hypotheses in the course of his study; and they yield data on the sequence of events from which the direction of causality may be more reliably inferred. Their serious weakness, however, is that the validity of inferences made from them is always subject to doubt." Given this weakness, it seems to us that a useful endeavor would entail the generation of data appropriate to an adequate test of the model's utility.

1
Introduction
The Community Under Stress

Perhaps the most basic issue in the application of sociological and organizational theory to human welfare is the nature of the relationship between human needs and the organizations society creates for their fulfillment. The human need in this study is food, and the organizations include the Seattle, Washington, welfare agencies and more directly, Neighbors in Need (NIN), an emergent organization which arose during an economic crisis in Seattle's recent history.

In this introductory chapter, we will illustrate the general economic climate and changes that took place in the Seattle area during the transition from economic boom to gross unemployment. Because of the inadequacy of existing normative systems to respond, the consequence was an unprecedented level of community need and hunger, which gave rise to an emergent organization, Neighbors in Need. Originally intended as a temporary organization that would disband as existing organizations assumed its duties, NIN underwent a colorful history characterized by a variety of structural and goal alterations as it sought to become a formalized and permanent community fixture.

In the ensuing chapters we turn our attention first to conceptualizing collective environmental stress situations, of which the economic alterations that occurred in Seattle are just one example. In the same chapter (Chapter Two) we also seek to detail the theoretical factors which comprise and define emergent organizations, such as NIN, as well as pose the basic theoretical questions raised in this text: (1) what factors and processes facilitate the persistence or demise of emergent organizations that form in periods of collective environmental stress? And (2) will such organizations, if they survive, compete or cooperate with existing agencies and organizations which possess similar tasks and functions? Having pieced together a general interpretative schema in Chapter Two, we then, in Chapter Three, present our data and its interpretation.

Chapter Three presents the basis for a series of propositions in the form of a causal model that predicts the persistence of emergent organizations. Environmental stress, community demands for service, organizational capacity, formalization and task orientations are identified and discussed as key factors in determining an organization's emergence, maintenance or demise. This analysis of the history of NIN, however, produces several insights beyond the model generated. In Chapter Four, we address these additional issues, namely, the effect of environmental alterations on changes in organizational goals and structures. Finally, in Chapter Five, we switch our attention from the theoretical to the practical and address the implications of our findings regarding the history of NIN for organizations which seek to service community needs.

Let us now, however, turn our attention to providing a general background for the economic milieu of the Seattle community and our focal organization, Neighbors in Need.

ECONOMIC CONDITIONS

During the 1965-68 period, the greater Seattle area experienced what can only be called an economic boom. A report by the Select Committee on Nutrition and Human Needs of the United State Senate (1971: 6) shows an increase of 170,000 persons employed over these years. Moreover, the unemployment rate in Washington remained relatively constant, averaging 4.3%. These favorable conditions were due in large part to the expansion and development of the aerospace industry, represented primarily by the Boeing Company in Seattle.

Beginning in 1969, however, a number of cutbacks by the government to the aerospace industry signalled an end to the boom. The unemployment rate rose to 4.8%, and by the end of January 1970, it had reached 10.1% without any indication of leveling off. In raw figures, the number of unemployed during the first three-quarters of 1970 went from 43,900 to 106,400 (Select Committee on Nutrition and Human Needs, 1971: 6).

From the beginning of the cutbacks until May 1971, the Boeing Company laid off 61,000 workers, and by June of 1971 Seattle's unemployment rate was registered as 15.7%. This turned out to be the highest unemployment rate for any metropolitan region in the United States, indicating the extent to which Seattle had become dependent upon the aerospace industry, and more specifically, the Boeing Company.

The situation as revealed through raw figures and percentages is only part of the picture. A closer look at the characteristics of the persons who were unemployed shows an even more bleak circumstance; e.g., males under thirty years of age constituted the greatest number of unemployed. This meant that young family heads were out of work, and since many of them had not been working long enough to build up a sufficient resource base to carry them over a period of retraining or relocation, they were caught in an economic crunch with no immediate way of extricating themselves. The maximum period of unemployment compensation was thirty-nine weeks. After that the "new poor" were on their own.

On the other side of the coin, those who had managed to acquire credit, savings accounts, insurance policies, and valuable possessions such as homes, automobiles, and boats found that they were ineligible for the existing public assistance programs. These persons, one in ten statistically, were left on their own from the beginning. Once their savings had been used up and their insurance policies cashed in, their predicament was similar to those having exhausted the unemployment compensation. Given the nature of the economy, the sale of personal possessions offered little promising relief. Indeed, the market was saturated with items of this type for sale.

Along with this group, single persons or childless couples between the ages of eighteen and fifty years of age were also ineligible for public assistance so long as they were employable. It didn't matter that there were no jobs available.

Some persons, on the other hand, were eligible for a small food allowance. The Food Stamp Program administered by the Department of Agriculture allowed persons to buy food stamps if they earned less than $195.00 a month, and had less than $1,500.00 in liquidable assets. From the outset of the unemployment situation until May 1971, there was an 18.2% increase in the use of the Food Stamp Program. This provides a crude indication of the number of persons whose incomes had dropped to the poverty level. Undoubtedly, this program was helpful to those who could afford to purchase the food stamps, but for many this was only sporadically possible because accidents and other unanticipated expenses frequently left them without the cash necessary to buy food stamps.

COMMUNITY HUNGER

The local newspapers, the Seattle Post Intelligencer and the Seattle Times, kept the public well posted on the rising unemployment and the demands for service for the public assistance facilities and social service agencies. An item reporting that the Red Cross had food available brought a crowd of two hundred and fifty, but unfortunately, there were supplies only for twenty-five. In July 1970, Mr. Emory Bundy, Public Affairs Director for KING Television and Radio approached Dr. William Cate, President of the Church Council of Greater Seattle, asking his opinion on the extent of human suffering. Dr. Cate questioned the council and began to gather information and identify needs. It was found that suffering did in fact exist, and had existed, especially in the black community, for some time. The biggest part of this suffering was related to hunger.

The members of the church agency staffs then moved out to meet with persons of the business sector, community organizations and social service agencies. It was believed that the government would eventually act to alleviate the suffering but that something still had to be done during the interim. It was also thought that the church agencies were the only body sufficiently large enough and properly motivated to undertake the task of feeding the hungry during the emergency that would exist until the government stepped in with a solution to the problem.

A model emergency relief program to be called *Neighbor's in Need* (NIN) was drawn up and presented on September 29, 1970, to the Church Council at its general assembly meeting. The program was to be based in the community, which would be divided into twenty to forty neighborhoods. Food collection and distribution points were to be located in these neighborhoods with each unit being staffed and organized by neighborhood local coordinators and other volunteers. Of course, there would also be some initial training for all coordinators and volunteers prior to getting under way with the operations.

News of the program was to be disseminated through the local media, pastors, church mailings, and community leaders. These reports would explain the crisis and define the needs in terms of their own areas. Food would be sorted, wrapped, and distributed by the trained volunteers. Each unit was to maintain a 10% reserve in order to handle sudden, unanticipated needs in their own or other stations. Records regarding the patterns of use were to be kept by the volunteers and coordinators in all stations. This was necessary in order to provide a basis for collection appeals.

The *Neighbors in Need* program was seen as a short-term (approximately six months) emergency service organization. Its goals were to (1) provide food for the unemployed, and (2) draw the attention of the public and the government to the problems of hunger in the area so that the public sector would be impelled to act (Taylor, 1971). This model was approved and adopted by the General Assembly of the Church Council, and, therefore, agency staff members immediately began to recruit the help of clergy in each neighborhood. These persons, then, with the help of their memberships, recruited volunteers and selected coordinators. The first group of approximately three hundred volunteers was ready for training on October 7, 1970.

One of the local ministers developed a set of training sessions to facilitate smooth operation of the independent units. Volunteers were informed that food was to be given to people simply because they expressed a need for it, and not because they "deserved" help—the prevailing attitude of the existing welfare agencies. Volunteers went through the process of filling out applications for public assistance and playing the role of applicants. The members of the training team played the role of the agency bureaucrats. When asked to give the one word relating their feelings about their role playing, the volunteers reported that they felt: "humiliated," "frustrated," "frightened,""alienated," "naked," etc. The role-playing exercise was used to make the point that having a need does not make a person less human. It was emphasized that the volunteers had neither the expertise nor the right to be evaluative in their dealings with NIN recipients. In addition, a number of techniques designed to make the recipients feel comfortable, welcome and respected were taught.

The guiding ideology of NIN, then, was, and continues to be, that food is to be given upon request. No proof of need is required, and the volunteers are to do whatever they can to reduce the strain and stigma of having to ask for assistance. They do not see this as giving out handouts; rather, it is a means of redistributing food from those who have a little extra to those who have none.

While the training sessions were going on, the local clergy were also busy locating collection and distribution centers which turned out to include churches, store fronts, and home basements. In addition, the food collection drive was initiated. Television, radio, newspapers, church publications, and word of mouth were used to inform the community of the existing state of hunger. After a period of ten days on October 17, 1970, thirty-four Neighbors in Need food banks were opened for business in the King County region.

It is significant that in only six weeks after the various church agencies realized the extent of the hunger problem, they had invented and implemented a radical and apparently successful organization to help feed the unemployed. We'll turn now to a closer inspection of the organization which will be necessary if we are to understand the reasons for their success.

ORGANIZATIONAL STRUCTURE AND OPERATIONS

During the first months of NIN's operation, each of the food banks was completely autonomous. Except for the 10% emergency reserve stock, food and money were collected locally and distributed locally. From October 1970 until October 1971, NIN was managed by a steering committee composed of members of the staffs of the founding agencies: Church Council of Greater Seattle, Ecumenical Metropolitan Ministry (EMM), Fellowship of Christian Urban Service and the churches of

Seattle. Responsibility for training volunteers and developing strategy was given to the EMM. It has been estimated that approximately one thousand volunteers were training during the first year. The Fellowship of Christian Urban Service administered the program, arranged for publicity, and handled telephone calls. It was not unusual for three hundred calls to be received on any given day. The Church Council of Greater Seattle answered correspondence, provided liaison with the three hundred plus churches participating in NIN, and managed the finances for the NIN trust fund. Funds for administrative expenses were drawn from pledges ranging from five hundred to two thousand dollars from a number of denominations. A full report of the money received and spent by the individual food banks is not available, and it would be impossible to estimate the value of food donations received since the inception of NIN. Perhaps we can get a better idea of the mode of organization by examining the day-to-day operations of one or two of the local units.

The Capitol Hill unit was set up by a church group called Churches Organized in Common Effort (CHOICE). Operations were carried out in a small house which was rented by a local church. The back rooms of the house were used for storage and packaging food, and the coordinator lived upstairs. It was initially staffed by members of CHOICE, but following the training period of volunteers, daily operations were assumed completely by volunteers. The unit was open for business at noon three days a week. People usually began lining up long before noon, so numbers were distributed on a first come, first served basis. The doors were opened at noon and the recipients were called in by number.

When the weather was warm, interviewers spent a few moments gathering information that would be helpful in continuing NIN operations. On cold or rainy days, however, this step was generally omitted since there was not enough room to have people waiting in line protected from the elements. In this case, the only information gathered was family size; and once this was known, the individuals were directed to stacks of boxes which had been prepacked in relation to family size. The amount of food issued also varied with the availability for any given day. When we asked how much food was allotted to each family, one of the volunteers commented: "That depends on how many people there are out there and how much food is in here. Usually it's too many out there or not enough in here." During the first year of operation, the Capitol Hill unit served an average of three hundred and fifty people per day.

Another unit located in a small Lutheran Church in one of Seattle's northern suburban areas revealed a different pattern of development. At first food was arranged on shelves as in a market and recipients simply selected items in accordance with their need. Four volunteers distributed food four hours a day, five days a week. This was possible in the beginning because there were fewer recipients in this area; by winter of 1970, however, the number of recipients had grown to such an extent that this method of distribution became cumbersome. At this point, a prepackage system similar to that of the Capitol Hill unit was adopted. By spring this unit was using two of the church's classrooms, one as a reception room and one for packaging and distributing food, as well as the pastor's office for storage. It also became necessary to adopt the Monday, Wednesday, Friday distribution schedule. The heavy demand and dual functions of collection and distribution made this type of scheduling necessary. In fact, at this time, most of the NIN units were operating in a similar fashion.

By the spring of 1971, a relatively stable group of volunteer personnel had filled the framework of Neighbors in Need. It was decided, therefore, that representatives of these personnel should be involved in the decision-making structure of NIN. Coordinators from the six geographical regions of King County were represented by the steering committee to elect two persons from their respective areas. These twelve representatives, then, assumed positions in the field operations committee. The field operations committee was designated to take over strategy and organizational development.

COMMUNITY RESPONSE TO NIN

Local television, radio, and newspapers provided supportive publicity to NIN. In addition, the religion editor of the Seattle

Times gave extended support in his column. The religion editor also spearheaded an all out Christmas collection which brought $176,000 to the NIN trust fund. Donations ran from coins given by children to more than one thousand dollars by certain organizations. Likewise, churches of all denominations held weekly food collections and conducted periodic drives, with the youth groups representing a particularly active segment of their population. Numerous families regularly donated a small quantity of food each week to their local unit. Interestingly, many of these donors expressed a desire to remain anonymous. It is known, however, that some donors later became recipients and some of the recipients were able to become donors. The reciprocal give and take characteristic of the period would seem to be a major factor contributing to NIN's early success.

In addition to the churches, other voluntary community organizations began to pitch in their help. Girl Scouts, Boy Scouts, Bluebirds, Campfire Girls, and Brownies made food collection a central part of their programs. Along with these efforts, a number of student bodies initiated school food drives, collecting thousands of canned and packaged foods as well as money donations. Furthermore, a massive food drive was conducted by certain state legislators, the local news media, business firms, and the Washington State Trucker's Association. Fire stations throughout the county served as collection points, and the National Guard offered its service in transporting much of the food to NIN units. This activity became known as "Operation Hunger" and continued to operate for several months.

A wide variety of work organizations became involved. Postal workers and city employees adopted a payroll deduction schedule. The Human Resources department of the City of Seattle estimated that payroll deductions provided up to $500.00 in one month. Farmers in eastern Washington donated large amounts of produce during the harvest seasons. The addition of fresh fruits and vegetables to the usual canned food allotments was well received. An abundance of odd sized potatoes was made available by the farmers, and became a NIN staple. These contributions were delivered to Seattle by volunteers using their own and borrowed trucks.

THE GOVERNMENT ACTS

The first year of operations found NIN busy coordinating its service with the community's supply and demand. There was no direct and overt appeal to the government during this period. Rather, it was assumed that the nature of the hunger, made apparent by the organization's success, would jolt the government into action. It did, but not in the direction envisioned by the early steering committee and the later membership. As stated in the report of the Select Committee on Nutrition and Human Needs (1971:8):

> The Legislature responded to increased demands on the Public Assistance Budget by tightening the qualifications for assistance and by revising the system under which the size of grants was determined. The Legislature claimed that the reforms would make more money available to those who were eligible for Public Assistance. The actual effect of the reforms was to reduce grants by an average of 15% principally by cutting the shelter allowance.

By the middle of April, NIN was already feeling the impact of this governmental action. Welfare recipients could not purchase food stamps without cash and, since they had to draw upon their food money for rent, they were turning to NIN. Thus, NIN was beginning to serve not only as an emergency or temporary source for food, but also as a supplementary source for persons who were already on welfare and unable to make ends meet with the standard agency grants. As might be expected, this turn of events precipitated some local political agitation. The Employment Coalition of Seattle arranged a meeting with the City Council, urging councilmen to become directly and actively involved in securing help for the city. While the meeting was in session, a welfare rights group simulated a temporary food distribution center just outside the Council Chambers in order to dramatize the increased demand resulting from the legislative cutbacks. Not long after this, Senators Jackson and Magnuson introduced a bill to amend the Public Works and Economic Development Act of 1965. This bill, the Economic Disaster Relief Act of 1971 (Congressional Record, May 5, 1971), would have established an emergency federal economic assistance program authorizing the President to declare certain areas of the nation under specific economic and employment criteria to be economic disaster areas and thus available for federal assistance. The Bill passed the Senate, but became bogged down in the House of Representatives. Two weeks after initiating this bill, Senator Magnuson, while speaking in support of a bill to improve the Food Stamp Act, made direct reference to the hunger situation in Seattle. Magnuson quoted a telegram sent by a minister on behalf of the United Presbyterian Synod of Washington-Alaska to the President informing him of the urgent need and requesting his help. This bill was likewise deferred. Governor Evans also requested the help of the federal government, but to no avail.

In July of 1971 the director of the Western Region, United States Department of Agriculture (USDA), along with his aides came to Seattle investigating requests by agencies of the state for a concurrent selling of food stamps and distribution of surplus commodities by the USDA. It was the stated opinion of the director that the Food Stamp Program was completely sufficient to meet the local situation. These representatives of USDA were provided with case histories of families who were not making it on the food stamp allotment, whereupon the director requested a number of government and public agencies to collect and compile hard data to support the State's case. Several days after the visit, the Office for Economic Services in the Washington State Department of Social and Health Services made a formal request for the concurrent programs. It was pointed out in this letter that the State of Washington would pay for the administration of two distributions and that precautions would be taken so that no single family would benefit simultaneously from both plans. The USDA replied that any type of dual operation could not be justified.

Requests for the release of surplus commodities by Governor Evans, Senator Magnuson, and Senator Percy (Illinois) similarly fell upon deaf ears. The Assistant Secretary of Agriculture also paid a visit to Seattle, where he met with both Governor Evans and the King County Executive. The Secretary, however, remained steadfast in refusing to release surplus commodities because there was no evidence that the Food Stamp Program was failing.

By fall a suit had been filed in the U.S. District Court on behalf of one poor person and other impoverished persons in the state requesting declaratory and injunctive action to keep the USDA from refusing to allow the concurrent operations of the commodity distribution and the Food Stamp Program. On December 6, 1971, United States District Judge William T. Beeks ruled in favor of this person, noting that the defendants were acting unlawfully in two ways: (1) the USDA policy against dual operations "was obviously in conflict with the intent of Congress," and (2) the refusal of the State request for dual operations was "arbitrary and capricious," representing an abuse of the discretionary power of the Secretary of Agriculture. The government response and the small court victory played a part in turning NIN from an apolitical helping organization to one that was more politically agressive.

THE POLITICALIZATION OF NIN

It was now apparent to the membership of NIN that the federal and state governments were not planning any large-scale aid to the Seattle area. Following the government welfare cutbacks and the concomitant increase in NIN recipients, those involved felt a sense of anger and frustration. One of the NIN board members in a letter to the Seattle Times expressed the sentiment of most when he stated that, "This (the feeding of the hungry) is a job for the government. It is our government. It's the government of the people who are hungry too." The volunteers could not close the distribution centers and ignore the thousands of hungry people that they were feeding. Thus, the membership began to develop a greater political awareness and the belief that NIN should enter into more direct confrontation with the government.

The increased hunger and the corresponding increase in the size of NIN operations lessened the efficiency of the loosely built autonomous distribution centers. A number of the major staple supplies had to be stored in a central location where easy access could be facilitated, especially for the centers in the central area where the demand had outstripped the local unit supply. Along with this development a system of bulk buying was arranged with a local grocery wholesaler. Space was initially found at a centrally located cathedral, and a warehouse manager was appointed. Soon, however, the scope of the food collection and purchasing made this arrangement unsuitable. At the request of Senator Ridder, the Port of Seattle agreed to allow NIN to use some of the warehouse space at Pier 91, and a full-time director was appointed.

There were also changes in the management of NIN. The field operations committee, recognizing that NIN was likely to continue operations indefinitely, felt that they should assume the full burden of decision making. This committee, with the support of the unit coordinators, decided to incorporate all the King County food distribution centers as Neighbors in Need, Inc., a nonprofit corporation with the field operations committee being designated as the board of directors. The reasons for incorporation included the desire to (1) protect the individual distribution centers and volunteers from possible liability suits, (2) achieve more central control of financial matters, and (3) create a legal entity in order to receive property such as trucks, which the city and county were prepared to lend. This decision on the part of the field operations committee resulted in the three agencies which had been represented on the steering committee withdrawing from a decision-making capacity.

Their relations with the new board of directors, however, remained friendly, and they assured NIN's leadership that their staffs would help in an advisory capacity if necessary. The first board of directors, as it turned out, did not constitute a representative cross-section of the various ethnic groups involved in NIN. Following an exchange with leaders of minority groups, therefore, it was decided that the board would be composed of sixteen members; four white Christians, four Blacks, two Indians, two Chicanos, two Jews, and two Asians. While these shifts in operations show an increase in NIN's political aggressiveness, the politicalization of NIN was also helped along with some international publicity and aid from a number of foreign countries.

To begin with, a minister on sabbatical leave from the United Church of Christ in Japan came to Seattle to observe the hunger problem. This person returned to Japan with a report on his observations. In response, a number of canned and packaged goods as well as over three hundred dollars in cash was sent to NIN from Japan. The money was used to purchase rice from a Japanese grower in California. Along with the representative from Japan, a member of the Lebanon and Palestinian Refugee Committee spent two weeks in Seattle also observing the hunger problem. This individual was impressed with the NIN operation and felt that more political involvement would be necessary. Following his return to Lebanon, this person sent NIN one hundred dollars on behalf of the Near East Council of Churches. In addition to these specific incidences, donations were received by NIN from many parts of the world: American servicemen, Canadians, Italians, Germans, and a couple in Holland each sent small contributions.

An interesting aspect of the overseas aid to NIN is that, apparently, it reflected negatively upon the United States government. In a speech to the United States Senate, Senator Magnuson stated, "I have served in the United States Senate for over twenty-five years and in all of that time I have never felt ashamed of my government. But today I stand on the floor of the greatest deliberative body in the world in total humiliation . . . in one simple, humanitarian gesture, Japan has made a mockery of our pious claims of being a nation dedicated to the cause of human dignity and the concern for the well-being of our citizens." Partly as a response to these developments, the USDA released some surplus commodities for distribution in Seattle. But as the News Director of KOMO Radio suggested in a broadcast on December 10, 1971: "It seems to me that the Department of Agriculture has not suddenly developed a heart. Rather, there is every reason to believe that fear of further embarrassment was the real cause of the policy reversal. It would be nice if the public could view the release of food as humanitarian...but one gets the nasty feeling that it was political. Anti-humanitarian actions are bad politics for only one reason..it's bad politics to be anti-people."

COMMUNITY STRESS: AN OVERVIEW

NIN had served 415,000 persons or 103,000 families with food during their first year of operation. Almost 90% of these people had applied for government help. Among these persons,

19% were waiting to be processed, 27% had been found ineligible, and 43% received some aid, but it was insufficient to meet their needs. This suggests that NIN emerged largely as a supplementary program to the existing agencies. An interesting question, therefore, is what happens when a supplementary program is no longer necessary? If NIN had emerged from and been sponsored by the existing agencies, the answer would be obvious: it would be phased out. But, as we have seen, NIN developed quite independently of the existing welfare systems. In addition, its emergence has raised questions in the minds of many persons. People want to know what is wrong with a system that can put men on the moon and develop power to destroy the world, but cannot arrange its priorities so that it can provide decent living conditions and the dignity of labor for its citizens. While a complete answer to these questions is clearly beyond the scope of the present text, it is believed that by approaching these events analytically and trying to explain sociologically what took place, we will gain some fruitful leads with respect to organizationally meeting the needs of our society. Therefore, having provided the reader with a general background detailing the economic events that occurred in Seattle, the needs these environmental changes provoked in the community at large, and the emergence of NIN to meet these needs, let us now proceed to Chapter Two, where we shall conceptualize collective environmental stress, detail those factors which comprise emergent organizations that develop in response to such stress, develop the general interpretative schema that will be used in the presentation and analysis of our finds in Chapter Three, and pose the basic theoretical questions which will be addressed by the text.

2
The Community as Environment for the Organizational Response

ENVIRONMENTS AND EMERGENT ORGANIZATIONS

Communities or any social systems that experience collective stress because of some type of rapid change in their environment (for example, major bombings or some other sort of disaster), seek to accommodate these disruptions through an infinite variety of modes (Barton, 1969: 274-275). One mode of coping that has been empirically documented in a number of different circumstances involving collective stress is group emergence. Such groups have been labeled with different titles such as "conflict groups," "accommodation groups" (Quarantelli, 1970: 2) and "emergent organizations" (Haas and Drabek, 1973: 6-7). Regardless of these labels, however, the inherent difference between these "emergent" groups or organizations and other organizations is that they do not exist prior to the stress circumstance and that they operate, at least initially, with relatively slight degrees of structural formality or behavioral continuity (Dynes, 1970: 138).

The vast majority of research on such emergent organizations suggests that they initiate their existence during periods of community or collective stress, fulfill unmet community functions by operating as transitory interaction systems, and then cease to exist, dissolving after the emergency or collective stress period has been terminated (Haas and Drabek, 1970: 6; Taylor, et al., 1970: 7, 9-108). Quarantelli (1970: 4), however, has illustrated that only " . . . some emergent groups cease to exist when the immediate crisis is over, whereas others become part of a new social order." The actual conditions that result in a certain group becoming a permanent and established organization,

Quarantelli (1970: 11) explains, " . . . rest on the new group being defined as one that carries out necessary tasks or activities not the traditional responsibility of already established groups or organizations."

Quarantelli's discourse is quite functional for describing some community changes which result from sudden impact stress agents such as bombings, earthquakes,tornadoes, and so on; however, it falls short of offering anything beyond providing a sensitization of the "climate" or circumstances which give rise to an emergent organization. This is a necessary first step, but it stands as wanting in that it does not facilitate the scientific goal of prediction, particularly with respect to the persistence of the organization. The actual mechanism which gives rise to an emergent group or organization and the means whereby such groups dissolve or turn into permanent parts of the community have actually received little attention in the literature.[1] This may be the case because research on this unique type of organization has placed its main attention on sudden onset, short-duration impact disasters, excluding for the most part the gradual onset, long-duration impact disasters (cf. Barton, 1969: 42-46).[2]

In the actual researching of disaster situations, social scientists seem to have given attention only to disasters that have been precipitated by the rapid onset of some hazard agent (Anderson, 1969: 16-23). Most existing research conclusions thereby apply to emergent organizations in this one kind of disaster setting. It may be that these efforts have been restricted in scope because of the immediacy of disaster situations and the specific interests of sponsoring agencies for practical implications relevant to emergency planning. Nevertheless, this focus has left open the question of whether or not different kinds of disaster stress situations impose different structural constraints on social behavior, and therefore on emergence and continuation of organizations and their development. The analysis of this question might well aid in lifting the disaster literature from its current descriptive stage to a more analytic one.

If generalizations that are relevant to all types of stress and disaster situations are to be achieved, the structural basis of group emergence and the detailing of those processes which facilitate the persistence of emergent organizations must be specified and systematically investigated across the full variety of collective stress situations. With this in mind, it seems realistic to assume that those mechanisms and processes which contribute to the persistence of such organizations will be more readily observed in long-term, progressively advancing disaster stress situations. The framework which will be used for interpreting findings has been provided by several recent environmental theorists.

AN INTERPRETATIVE SCHEMA

Emery and Trist (1972: 275) have proposed that increasing rates of change among several environments external to an organization, even though these may not be directly connected to the organization through its actual inputs and outputs, will have dramatic consequences for processes internal to the organization (cf. Terreberry, 1968; Mileti and Gillespie, 1976). Their perspective indicates that an organization which is surrounded by a "turbulent field" will increase behavior directed toward maximizing the survival of the organization, and, correspondingly, decrease goal achieving behavior. Hall (1972: 302) corroborates this assertion by noting that, "in periods of economic distress, an organization is likely to cut back or eliminate those programs it feels are least important to its overall goals."

If these theorists are correct, it would seem to produce a paradox among welfare agencies: in time of economic distress the need for welfare can be expected to increase, yet the established agencies will shrink from meeting this need or "output goal" and, instead, shift to an emphasis on survival maintenance.[3] This, then, would seem to create an area of unmet community needs with respect to the welfare of the inhabitants of a given area. Such unmet needs are likely to prompt the formation of a new organization (Parr, 1970: 429). Indeed, Neighbors in Need was one such organization which was organized in response to general economic distress in a community as a distributor of bulk food to Seattle's hungry population. In brief, NIN began operation in November 1970 as a concerned community group attempting to fill the gaps in public assistance;

other welfare agencies were simply unwilling to meet the increased demands brought about by onset of high unemployment in the community.

This development suggests an important theoretical question: will organizations of this type, once established, seek to compete or cooperate with existing agencies, and, of equal importance, will they be co-opted or legitimated as independent units? Levine and White (1972) and Evan (1972) have each proposed theoretical frameworks in response to this question. While these theorists are in agreement on certain issues, they are unclear and in disagreement on others. It may be assumed that the area of disagreement represents the weakest link in each of these theories. Therefore interpretation of our data will focus most crucially upon this aspect of the theories. A brief outline of each theory will now be presented, followed by a specification of their agreements and disagreements regarding interorganizational relations.

Levine and White studied the interrelations among health organizations. They defined cooperation as an organizational exchange, which is considered to be "any voluntary activity between two organizations which has consequences, actual or anticipated, for the realization of their respective goals or objectives" (1972:344). Organizations cooperate by exchanging elements, which among health organizations include cases, employees, funds, equipment, and information.

Levine and White (1972: 345-352) present several determinants of exchange. If an organization is dependent upon support provided by a given set of organizations, it is likely to seek exchanges with those organizations. Levine and White (1972: 346), in support of this claim, found that corporate organizations with connections outside the community were less likely to interact with local agencies. An organization's functions are another determinant of exchange. Some organizations have functions which can be discharged more or less independently, while others require frequent interaction with various organizations. They report that agencies with direct service functions were more likely to enter into exchanges than agencies providing indirect services (1972: 349). NIN and other welfare agencies obviously represent direct service functions. A third factor for exchange is "domain consensus" by which the authors mean interorganizational agreements concerning respective goals and functions (1972: 352). With NIN and the welfare agencies these agreements would include the community's (a) need for food, (b) members served, and (c) services rendered. Unless consensus can be achieved, competition rather than cooperation would be anticipated according to Levine and White.

We now turn to a brief consideration of Evan's work. Evan (1972:329) made this extension by introducing the concept of organizational set. Analysis is then focused upon interactions between a given organization ("the focal organization") and other organizations within the set (1972: 329). Within this framework, it is suggested that the role-set of "boundary personnel" provide an indication of interorganizational relations. Interorganizational cooperation, therefore, may be conceived as transactions occurring within role-sets of boundary personnel.

Evan (1972: 332-336) suggests several hypotheses concerning the factors which determine the nature of interorganizational relations. First, Evan's (1972: 333) theory predicts that, if there is goal similarity between the focal organization and the members of its set, they will compete rather than cooperate. However, with an overlap in membership, the hypothesis is reversed, with the combinatorial effects of goal similarity and overlapping membership leading to cooperation.

The theory predicts secondly that complementarity of functions between the focal organization and its role-set members results in "cooperative actions" (1972: 335). NIN and the local welfare agencies may on this basis be expected to cooperate. Further, if the focal organization suffers a "shortage of input resources" (1972: 336) it is more likely to cooperate with the input organizations in its set. The input organizations are those which provide the focal organization with its resources, for example, funds, people, and legitimacy.

Both Levine and White and Evan agree that some control over, and a shortage of, resources are a prerequisite to interorganizational cooperation. Cooperation, seen in this light, is a mechanism for relieving shortages. Resource shortage, however, may be said to be a necessary but not sufficient condition for cooperative behavior. An organization lacking resources for goal attainment may avert the difficulty simply by the designation of a new goal. At what point a particular organization might change its goals rather than interact with another organization is a prediction not ventured by these theorists. Furthermore, while Levine and White postulate mutual acceptance of one another's goal as a necessary condition for cooperation, Evan views goal similarity as a condition for competition. While it would appear that Levine and White and Evan advance opposite predictions—Levine and White predicting cooperation and Evan predicting competition—this, in fact, is not the case. Levine and White would argue that similarity of functions between NIN and the other welfare agencies does exist; however, as Whetten (1975:10) points out, domain consensus refers not only to agreements concerning goals and functions but also to who should carry these out. Therefore, Levine and White would predict competition on the basis of the fact that even though consensus exists on the first two factors of domain consensus it doesn't exist on the third factor: expectations about who should carry out the functions. As a result, both Levine and White and Evan would predict competition.[4]

The data produced from NIN and the Seattle Welfare Agencies (NIN's role-set members) indicate at this time tentative support for both Levine and White's and Evan's theories. In Chapter Three, the presentation of our data concerning NIN will be framed in terms of the environmental factors of change and demands for service as well as the organizational factors of capacity, formalization, and task orientation. These variables will be shown to be key dimensions in predicting the emergence, maintenance, or demise of an organization.

3
Organizational Persistence and Development During Community Stress

This chapter will present a series of propositions in the form of a causal model which facilitates prediction of the persistence of emergent organizations. Environmental change, community demands for service, organizational capacity, formalization, and task orientations are identified and discussed as important dimensions in determining the probability of organizational emergence, maintenance, or demise. It will be shown that NIN's career pattern shows a persistence beyond the period of environmental disruption because of the long-term progressive nature of stress imposed on the community system, NIN's formalization, and its task specificity. But a reduction in system stress, the adoption of a more diffuse goal, and the organization's failure to promote interorganizational relations with the local agencies results in some interesting developments and predictions regarding NIN's overall long-term persistence.

In Chapter Two we pieced together an interpretative schema based upon the theoretical works of Emery and Trist (1972), and Hall (1972). It will be remembered that their argument suggested that an organization surrounded by a "turbulent field" will increase survival behavior and, correspondingly, decrease goal directed behavior; and that we stated that the development of a "turbulent environment" seems to produce a paradox among welfare agencies. That is, in time of economic distress the need for welfare can be expected to increase, yet the established agencies will shrink from meeting this need and, instead, shift to an emphasis on survival maintenance. This organizational behavior then would appear to create an area of unmet needs with respect to the welfare of the inhabitants of a given population. It is on the basis of this framework that the first proposition is advanced: *The larger the environmental change, the greater the discrepancy between the organizational services provided by existing organizations and community demands for service.*

The degree of stress which is imposed by the environment may be large either in terms of actual intensity, or in terms of the proportion of the community affected. Research, as previously mentioned, has unilaterally been on the intense and dramatic impacts created by natural disasters. However, if established task domains are disrupted, the extent of the impact or the proportions of the system affected may be viewed as creating comparable collective stress situations from other types of precipitating agents. It was in this sense that alterations in the economic environment of Seattle were taken as generating a collective stress situation.

For a five year period, the expansion of the aerospace industry, during the years 1965 through 1969, led the city of Seattle into a period of economic prosperity. Unemployment was at its lowest level since World War II, with the general effect of shrinking the number of persons receiving welfare assistance and increasing the quantity of consumer credit purchases. The unemployment rate was both steady and low; it averaged about 4.3 percent during this period (Select Committee on Nutrition and Human Needs, 1971: 6). These factors contributed to an optimistic outlook with respect to the market, as well as reinforced the "boom" aspects of this period of prosperity.

The primary responsibility for the expansion of the aerospace industry in the area was the Boeing Corporation. Boeing provided many energizing inputs (Katz and Kahn, 1972) for the community social system as a whole which facilitated the operation of the system at high levels of output. As a result of changes in federal policy, however, a series of cutbacks in expenditures for aerospace research and development began in 1969. In response to these policy alterations, Boeing was forced to begin trimming its operations. This resulted in what was to become a massive decrease in the number of persons employed by the plant in the Seattle area. That is, the community system to a considerable extent, lost a major source of its inputs.

By the middle of 1969 the unemployment rate in Seattle rose to 4.8 percent. In January of 1970, the rate was 10.1 percent, and it continued to rise, reaching a high of 15.7 percent in June of 1971. Much of the increase in unemployment was attributable to the increasing impact and side effects of the cutbacks at Boeing. Boeing terminated more than one-half of its employees, showing a decrease from 106,000 employees in 1968 to 45,000 in 1971 (Select Committee on Nutrition and Human Needs, 1971: 5) in just three years. Males aged 25 years and under were those who experienced the largest increases in unemployment, but the toll among middle-age categories was almost as heavy. All this meant, in any regard, that a sizeable number of heads of families were unemployed.

The ability of the existing welfare system to adjust to and handle this change was regulated by normative anticipations of environmental demands, based largely on prior experience. Once again, drawing upon Emery and Trist (1972: 275), and Hall's (1972: 302) predictions regarding the shift from goal attainment to survival maintenance, it seemed very likely that a certain portion of the increased community needs and demands generated by the environmental change would remain unmet. That is, whether the stress agent's impact is immediate, as it is in most natural disasters, or progressive, there is a point beyond which the adaptability of the system is unable to meet the increased demand level. Our second proposition therefore asserts that, *the larger the environmental change, the less likely the normative system will be able to meet all of the community demands.*

There were two basic system mechanisms instigated to deal with unemployment and its associated problems and restore a "dynamic equilibrium" (Buckley, 1967: 36-40): unemployment insurance and public assistance. Many of those who now found themselves unemployed resorted to unemployment insurance as a means of survival while seeking new jobs. However, this insurance is payable only for a maximum of thirty-nine weeks, and the job market was closed for all practical purposes. As a result many families were soon forced to seek public welfare assistance. The normative ability of the community system to adapt to the increased demand was constrained in two ways.

First, because of bureaucratic inflexibility and limited resources, public assistance agencies were simply not prepared to handle an increased demand of this magnitude. Second, there were problems of eligibility. Many of the families which required assistance had acquired a great deal of material goods during the prosperity period which, in accordance with welfare normative operating standards, rendered them ineligible for the aid which they now so desperately sought. The sale of personal belongings did little more than irritate the problem, as the market was flooded with "must sell" goods. Many families, therefore, were ineligible for public assistance, and even those who were eligible for public aid faced waiting periods as long as six weeks without an income while eligibility interviews were held and applications processed.

For all practical purposes, Seattle was experiencing collective stress generated by forces external to the social system (Barton, 1969: 38-48). The situation, furthermore, was characterized as progressive onset, long-duration impact and a low level of social preparedness. One could easily argue that it was the low level of community preparedness for the event and not the size of the impact which hindered the fulfillment of community demands. This, however, is doubtful because it must be acknowledged that with an established set of personnel to handle clients, the capacity of normative systems to adapt to change remains limited, irrespective of the level of preparedness.

Several factors limit the degree to which preparedness can upgrade a community's ability to adapt. Initially, the kind and degree of environmental alteration can never be completely anticipated. This is exacerbated with collective stress situations brought on by progressive impact disaster agents because there appears to be a tendency among the members of an afflicted population to construct temporary, makeshift ideologies which bolster the community's optimism regarding the creation of immediate relief and a quick solution to the stress situation. (Cantril, 1941: 139-143; Festinger et al., 1959: 193-215; Klapp, 1969: 3-21). In addition, Dynes (1970) suggests that communities anticipate future environmental change primarily in terms of past events and experience (Mileti et al., 1975). Communities which have experience with floods for example, will prepare for future floods by building flood banks or dikes just a few inches above the water level reached with the past event (Mileti, 1975). Finally, the effectiveness of community preparedness in allowing the system to respond more appropriately to the stress situation varies with such things as the time of day for rapid impact disaster, or the season of year for long-duration disasters. In Seattle, for example, the job market was further tightened when the school system slowed operations during the summer months: a significant segment of students seeking temporary employment was released into the community.

All of the factors thus far illustrated, involving physical, social, and symbolic constraints on the ability of the community system to adapt to external change, functioned to preserve particular unmet community demands for service in Seattle. It appears, then, that the intensity or magnitude of the environmental impact would be inversely related to the degree to which community or system normative adaptability can cope with the stress situation. This suggests that external change of certain intensities or durations will create demands for service which cannot or will not be met instrumentally by the established system. This was certainly the case with the welfare system in Seattle.

ORGANIZATIONAL BIRTH AND OPERATION

Research to date portrays emergent organizations as task oriented, loosely structured, traditionless, and short-lived groups. It has been suggested by Quarantelli (1970: 2) that such organizations emerge in an effort to accommodate the needs of a system under stress. Arnold Parr (1970) also reports that emergent organizations typically arise to meet unmet community needs which result from excessive demands that are placed on existing organizations, and that they disband when these demands decline. Parr (1970: 429) concluded that, "group emergence is one means through which community social systems cope with crises." This implies, regardless of the speed of onset connected with the precipitating disaster agent, that the generation of emergent groups is a response which would be common to all communities undergoing collective stress.

Proposition three therefore states that, *the larger the number of community demands, the more likely is the creation of an emergent organization.* The data from NIN to be presented support this contention.

An investigation of community problems was begun in July of 1969, following an inquiry of a local television official, by the Church Council of Greater Seattle. Several other religious organizations, the Ecumenical Metropolitan Ministry and the Fellowship of Christian Urban Service, were contacted and also contributed to the study and the assessment of the problem. Representatives of these church agencies met with heads of community service organizations, welfare administrators and various business leaders in an effort to determine what might be an appropriate course of action that the community might take in response to the prevailing conditions. In this assessment of the problem, it was assumed that the governmental intervention to provide relief would not be quick in coming; it would take time. Consequently, it was decided that an emergency relief program on the local level was necessary to sustain the community until the government was able to take some course of action.

Neighbors in Need (NIN) was the relief program that resulted. Initial support for the program and a steering committee was drawn from the membership of the three churches that were involved. Taylor (1971) points out that Neighbors in Need was envisioned and designed to be a short-term, emergency service organization. It was estimated that it would exist for about six months. NIN had two goals: (1) to provide food for the unemployed; and (2) to draw the attention of the public and the government to the problems of hunger in the area so that the public sector would be impelled to act. NIN thus began as an organization with only a slight administrative hierarchy, claiming distinct tasks and drawing upon existing organizations for its personnel funds.

The actual way that NIN emerged was strikingly similar to the descriptions of group behavior under sudden onset, short-duration impact disaster situations (Forrest, 1973). However, Dynes (1970: 138) states that since emergent groups are not formalized, it may be "inappropriate to label them organizations." Cautions of this type may be warranted when the extent of time between an environmental impact and the response of existing organizations is short. But in the case of gradual onset, prolonged impact disasters the time element becomes extended and this is crucially important. The presence of an extended time-lag between the actual impact of the environmental agent causing the stress situation and the response on the part of the established organizations facilitates an increase in information exchange and interaction patterns among community members. The development of communication links and the presence of new interaction patterns between community members are listed by Barton (1969: 216-279) as two key factors for "therapeutic community response."[5] They are critical in that such a response provides the foundation for the support of organizations to deal with the plight of the community and, assuming that commitments typically increase over time, it can be inferred that the gradual onset, prolonged impact disasters are structurally more conducive to the generation of formal structure, than are the sudden onset, short-duration disasters. Researchers studying organized behavior in disaster, therefore, should be alert to the social structural variations which emerge as a function of the speed or rate of change associated with the environmental impact of the disaster agent which is the cause of the collective stress situation.

In a mode similar to emergent organizations in short-term onset disasters, NIN was dependent upon the church and business sectors of the community for personnel. Because of the lack of resources and the absence of salaried positions in the organization, it was thought that the only successful tactic would be to evolve a "grassroots" base, and use most of the acquired funds to obtain food. As a result, the steering committee subdivided the Seattle area into neighborhoods which were to represent the bases of operation. Distribution and storage centers, called "food banks," were begun in each neighborhood and volunteers to staff the banks were recruited from local residents. It should be noted that the number of neighborhoods and food banks has varied greatly over time. Initially, thirty-four neighborhoods were distinguished, but by October 1972 there were sixty-nine banks in operations. The physical space for the food banks was either donated or rented for the cost of the utilities. This condition greatly enhanced the propensity for food mobility. If the cost of operating a particular food bank becomes too high or a donor reclaimed his space, a new donor or a less expensive location was sought and the food bank was moved to the new location. This ability to be mobile greatly facilitated autonomy with respect to the food bank's relations to the steering committee.

Because of this autonomy, the structure of NIN was and remains divided. The organization's administration (the steering committee) dealt with the acquisition of large contributions, liaison problems with the government and business sectors, keeping necessary records, and the coordination of the food banks' efforts, while acting as a source of emergency goods in the event that any particular food bank was temporarily unable to meet the demands made upon it. Individual food banks, however, assumed the tasks of canvassing for money and food contributions, and the distribution of goods. Each food bank had a "coordinating volunteer" who had the responsibility for keeping the NIN administration informed. This person was generally responsible for the overall operation of the bank as well.

It was the "grass-roots" strategy that was clearly responsible for this split organizational structure. While it is difficult to generalize to other organizations, this particular structure contributed to the continued existence of the organization. The relative autonomy of the individual banks freed the administration of concerns with day-to-day operations. Administrative efforts were initially freed to be directed to public relations, task refinements, task attainment strategies, and other concerns which had the effect of strengthening the organization.

FORMALIZATION OF THE EMERGENT ORGANIZATION AND ITS IMPACT ON COMMUNITY NEEDS

The degree of formalization and the relative success of providing for community problems achieved by a new organization both are largely contingent on the length of the time-lag between the emergence of the organization and the initial response of existing organizations (Chapin and Tsouderos, 1956;

Adler, 1965: 592-597). Also, the efforts of a new emergent organization are likely to be more poorly coordinated and less effective than those of organizations which already exist. This general ineffectiveness is most likely a function of the (1) lack of clearly elaborated and interrelated statements of goals, (2) absence of clearly defined centers of power, (3) lack of equipment and trained personnel, and (4) absence of a developed administrative structure. It is important to note that the presence of these conditions correlates positively with the short period of time that a new organization has been in existence. Therefore, the goals of the new and existing organizations should be expected to absorb the personnel of existing organizations, leaving the newly emerged organization without an operating base. When the time of impact is prolonged, however, existing organizations shift to survival maintenance (Hall, 1972: 302), providing an opportunity for new organizations to gain footing and formalize.

The emergence of new organizations is contingent upon the presence of certain conditions in the community social structure (Parr, 1970: 424-427; Lotz and Gillespie, 1972: 18-20), and a prolonged distress situation *per se* generates conditions which enhance the likelihood of formalization. It is not that all emergent organizations under such conditions will formalize, but that formalization is an alternative to being absorbed by existing organizations. In addition, new organizations are likely to resist being absorbed because their structure is less specialized or segmented, and they are serving a presumed community need which frequently leads to organizational solidarity and a desire to preserve the organization (cf. Tsouderos, 1955: 208-209).

NIN drew most of its donations and volunteers from Seattle area churches when it was first established. It was a new organization which was designed to operate only until the government was able to respond with a solution to the economic distress plaguing the Seattle area. Its objectives and goals were specific to the task at hand and questions of how to accomplish its goals were clear. Most administrators and workers were volunteers who served on an irregular basis. NIN conformed to descriptions of emergent organizations and provided built-in mechanisms for its own dissolution, anticipating that the existing organizations would respond positively within six months.

However, NIN had been in operation for eight months by April of 1971 and the administrators were becoming skeptical about being able to phase-out NIN quickly when a government solution to the hunger problem emerged. In mid-April, the state government did react. As described in NIN records:

> The legislature responded to increased demands on the Public Assistance budget by tightening the qualifications for assistance and by revising the system under which the size of grants was determined . . . . Welfare recipients had to use their food allowances for rent, could not buy Food Stamps without cash, and came to Neighbors in Need for help. The program was becoming not only a primary source of food for those in temporary need but also a supplementary source for families who could no longer feed themselves adequately on their welfare grants . . . . (Taylor, 1971:8).

This circumstance is exactly what the model thus far developed would have predicted; an increase in survival behavior and a decrease in goal achieving behavior on the part of the established organizations. The result was unmet community demands giving impetus to the creation of an emergent organization.

We may now extend the model by postulating that the specific task orientation of an emergent organization is likely to produce high initial success in meeting the community's demand for service. Proposition four, then, claims that, *as emergent organizations perform their task, the number of community demands decreases.*[6] If one were to extrapolate from the existing literature on emergent organizations, one would predict that as the unmet community demands are met, the likelihood of the new organization formalizing and persisting would decrease; that is, the emergent organization would be expected to die. However, as was pointed out earlier, the presence of an extended time-lag between external impacts and the appropriate response on the part of established organizations facilitates an increase in information exchange and interaction patterns among community organizations. This, in turn, increases the likelihood that the emergent organization will formalize; assuming that the longer information is being exchanged, the more likely it is that community needs and problems still exist. If so, the emergent organization will have a stake in legitimizing its operation. This implies the fifth and final proposition of the model: *the more an emergent organization formalizes, the greater the probability it will persist.* A primary variable in predicting the dissolution or persistence of an emergent organization, therefore, is the extent of that organization's success at formalization, and formalization is directly related to the number of community demands over time. The activities surrounding NIN's formalization substantiate the viability of the model as presented.

The actual cutbacks which were made by the state government had a major impact on NIN as an emergent organization. The size of NIN's client population expanded, requiring more volunteer personnel and dictating the addition of paid staff employees to labor full-time at the enlarged record keeping and information processing tasks. In addition, the cutbacks shattered the idea that NIN would soon be relieved of its duties. This marks the significant turning point for NIN, because it represents the first time a change in organizational strategy was required. The administration of NIN argued that either a failure could be declared and the organization dismantled, or a commitment to operate indefinitely without outside help would have to be made. The latter strategy was adopted and with it began the rapid formalization process.

NIN expanded the scope of its goals and assumed a posture much like that of a social movement organization in order to implement this change in strategy (Zald and Ash, 1966; Lotz and Gillespie, 1972: 14-15). The central purpose now became to "feed the hungry" and tactics were employed which reflected the greater breadth of the new goal. Massive donation drives were begun and a NIN trust fund was established. Regular canvassing procedures were outlined and the organization prepared to become more financially stable. However, numerous problems began to arise in connection with the receipt of large quantities of money and goods on behalf of the organization when increased donations were sought. Hence, an additional structural change in the organization was required.

The organization incorporated as a nonprofit one, with a board of directors, in May of 1971. Conflict plagued this act. The executive committee which had been administering NIN was at odds with the steering committee over various strategy changes. The act of incorporation served to formally sever the bond between church help and NIN, which established the emergent organization as an independent entity. Aside from solving problems of the acceptance of goods and money for the organization, incorporation facilitated the adoption of new tactics with respect to the acquisition of aid for the organization. NIN gained legal status and efforts to obtain federal surplus monies through the court system began. These legal maneuvers were initially treated as of secondary importance. The primary goal was held to be that of providing food for the community. The organizational change and legal activities, however, later assumed a more important role.

NIN flourished in the months following incorporation, with the number of clients continuing to grow and donations expanding. A system of bulk buying was instituted to decrease operation costs. Purchasing food in quantity introduced storage problems and NIN obtained use of government warehouse facilities. However, the acquisition of a warehouse required the addition of a paid director and helpers for the existing NIN staff. While most personnel were still volunteers, NIN had grown from a small all volunteer agency with sparse funding to one of the largest food distributors' organizations in the region.

Another series of events contributed to NIN's stabilization. During the period that NIN was formalizing, the unemployment problem in Seattle began to wane. Many who were rendered unemployed by Boeing and other firms left the state to seek work elsewhere. As people left, the economy began to rally and the number who were left unemployed as a result of the earlier distress began to shrink. Theoretically this should have also decreased the number of people using NIN, but it did not. Instead, the number of clients seeking the services of NIN continued to expand. Remembering that NIN had begun to pick up welfare recipients and other poor who used the services as a supplement to other aid, the growing number of clients is not hard to explain. NIN, as a supplier of food had evolved an extremely efficient structure and began to compete with established welfare agencies for clients.

The service NIN began to perform as a function of the economic distress also turned out to be a service important to the community under less distressing conditions. NIN's operation had revealed a heretofore latent community problem. This discovery apparently took place because of inefficiency connected with the normative system. As Williams (1971: 3) states, "of the households served by Neighbors in Need, fully 89 percent stated that they had *already* applied to one or more governmental programs for help. That these families found it necessary to seek assistance from NIN indicates that the existing governmental programs did *not,* in fact, provide the adequate or immediate aid required . . . ." Thus, without conscious design on the part of organizational leaders, NIN had begun a change of status from that of an emergency organization to a regular agency, primarily because a day-to-day pre-stress situation community problem was not being serviced.

This new stabilization was made easier by the previously described alteration in organizational goals and the subsequent focus on the more general problem of hunger. Note that when the emergency phase had passed and the leaders of NIN found themselves faced with a still growing operation, the attention given the anti-hunger ideology increased. Concern was no longer with feeding the unemployed but with simply feeding anyone who was hungry. In fulfilling this broader welfare function, the new emphasis on the more diffuse goal was further reinforced by the need to expand NIN's resource base.

The major result of the need to broaden the resource base was a rapid expansion of the organization. Beginning in the summer of 1971, a statewide coalition of private helping agencies was formed, still bearing the name of Neighbors in Need. By February 1972, sixty-nine food banks distributed over sixteen counties in the state of Washington were in operation. The attack on the hunger problem now included not only massive food distribution but also political pressure. NIN launched a number of court actions designed to promote the improvement and expansion of the welfare efforts in the state of Washington.

NIN was understandably plagued by problems of finance following this sizeable growth of the organization. Obtaining donations of cash and food from the public became difficult once the emergency period of the economic depression had passed. People were no longer willing to donate as much, nor as frequently, when the presence of a direct threat was no longer felt. The vast unemployment which had formed the basis for an effective appeal for donations had disappeared. The further tightening of the federal budget, coupled with the shrinking size of private donations leaves the future of NIN available for theoretical prediction.

A PREDICTION OF THE FUTURE

The case of NIN has shown that the progressive magnitude of an environmental impact, unemployment, rendered the welfare system unable to cope with the drastic change in inputs. As a consequence, there was an increase in the number of demands for service within the community system. The magnitude of the impact, furthermore, was found to be inversely related to the community system's normative adaptability. This was primarily a result of preparatory limitations within the welfare system which involved organizational optimism, rigid reliance on past experience, and constraints brought on with seasonal variation in the community school system. These limitations hindered the welfare system's ability to handle the hunger problem adequately.

Because unmet demands existed in the community system, an emergent organization was formed. NIN emerged as an organization with the short-range goals of providing immediate service for a faltering community system. NIN was initially a situational organization in that its projected lifespan was short. With only one exception, the extended time-lag, NIN conformed to the life cycle of emergent organizations described by Dynes (1970). In extrapolating from existing disaster research, then, NIN should have continued to function until existing agencies intervened and then dissolved, or have been absorbed by the existing organization. Such a course of events had been observed during sudden onset, short-duration impact disasters, but the life cycle of NIN is an exception.

The organization proved to be an exception because its operations had uncovered a latent hunger problem which existed within the normal day-to-day functioning of the system. This disclosure facilitated NIN's continued existence after the period of distress had passed. Furthermore, the social processes connected with the time extension facilitated an increase in the formalization of the organization. Other things being equal, this development would lead one to predict that the organization will persist. But "other things" are rarely equal and, as it turns out, NIN's future remains precarious.

Although the goals of NIN and the established welfare agencies are similar, NIN's operational procedures are actually very different from those of the established system. NIN handles bulk food and distributes it through the use of minimally trained manpower. The established welfare system is characterized as a bureaucratic structure, employing trained personnel, and emphasizing the processing of clients through the use of rules and regulations. A number of studies have shown bureaucratic structures to be the most effective mode of organization during periods of environmental stability (Woodward, 1965; Lawrence and Lorsch, 1967; Rushing, 1968; Hage and Aiken, 1969; Palumbo, 1969). However, NIN's view of the local welfare system was formed during a period of environmental disruption, when the rigidity of bureaucracy reduces its effectiveness. Thus, rather than seeking to promote interorganizational relations with the local welfare agencies, NIN turned to the federal government (cf. Whetten, 1975: 9).

This response made it clear that continued operations were contingent upon NIN's ability to convince the federal government that its program supplemented and did not duplicate the existing services. It is not surprising, therefore, that following their temporary success with the federal government, NIN launched a campaign to promote the support of the community, and to bring the pressure of public opinion to bear upon the appropriate legislative bodies. This strategy turned out to be successful: in March 1974, OEO again allocated sufficient money to ensure another year of NIN operations. While the emergence and development of NIN has been in many respects unique, the findings nevertheless offer tentative support for

Levine and White's and Evan's contentions that resource shortage and disagreement on a portion of domain consensus (who should carry out the function) produce interorganizational competition. In addition, they suggest a formal model predicting organizational emergence and persistence.

The temporal model generated in this analysis for the emergence, formalization and persistence of emergent organizations in collective community stress situations is presented in Figure 1. By way of summary, the model integrates the propositions presented on the basis of data obtained in reference to Neighbors in Need in prior sections of this chapter.

FIGURE 1

A Temporal Model for the Emergence, Formalization and Persistence of Emergent Organizations

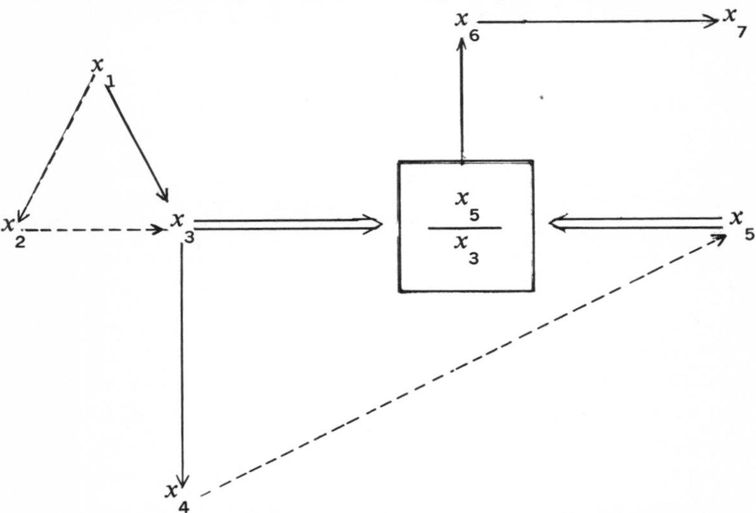

Where x_1 = magnitude of the event; x_2 = adaptability of the normative system; x_3 = system needs at time one (T_1); x_4 = organizational emergence; x_5 = systems needs at time two (T_2); x_6 = formalization; x_7 = organizational persistence; x_5/x_3 = index of change in system needs, where $x_5/x_3 \geq 1$ indicates formalization, and $x_5/x_3 < 1$ indicates dissipation; $\Longrightarrow$ indicates noncausal temporal paths.

The model suggests that the larger the magnitude of the disaster event (x_1) precipitating the collective stress situation, the less the ability of the normative community system to adapt (x_2) to the situation. It also states that the greater the magnitude of the event (x_1), the greater will be the volume of community system needs (x_3); and the less the ability of the normative system to adapt (x_2), the greater will be the volume of needs in the community system (x_3). System needs (x_3) is directly related to organizational emergence (x_4) which, in turn, decreases the volume of system needs, as that emergent organization performs its tasks, at some future point in time (x_5). The ratio of change

FIGURE 2
A Causal Model for the Emergence, Formalization and Persistence of Emergent Organizations

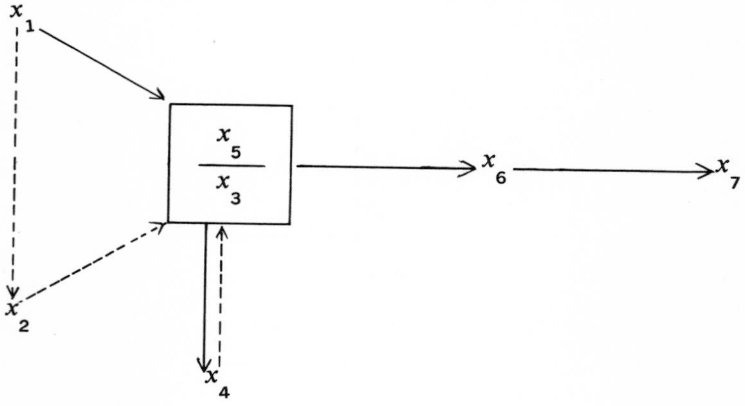

Where: x_1 = magnitude of the event; x_2 = adaptability of the normative system; x_3 = system needs at time one (T_1); x_4 = organizational emergence; x_5 = system needs at time two (T_2); x_6 = formalization; x_7 = organizational persistence; x_5/x_3 = index of change in system needs, where $x_5/x_3 \geq 1$ indicates formalization, and $x_5/x_3 < 1$ indicates dissipation.

in system needs to time (x_5/x_3) is the key factor which determines the formalization of the emergent organization. Formalization will occur if system needs grow while dissipation of the emergent organization is likely if system needs wane over time. Finally, formalization (x_6) is seen as the instrumental factor in predicting organizational persistence (x_7) as a permanent community organization emerging from the collective stress situation. Figure 2 is a causal representation of this same model with temporal paths excluded, illustrating the central role of the index of change in system needs as the key variable in predicting organizational emergence, formalization and persistence. However, our analysis of the career of NIN has produced insights beyond those presented in this chapter, namely, the effect of environmental alterations on changes in organizational goals and structure. This is the topic for Chapter Four.

4 Commitment and Transformation: Responses of the Rank and File

The concept of organizational goals has been central to the analysis of formal organizations. This is not surprising since, as Gross (1969: 277) notes, "it is the dominating presence of a goal which marks off the 'organization' from other kinds of systems." What is surprising, however, is that much of the research has focused exclusively on the goals of management, assuming organizations to perform as unified wholes. For example, a number of studies in this tradition have examined the nature of organizational response to environmental changes, showing the process of goal attainment to be similar to an adaptive organism adjusting to and compromising with its environment; that is, the values and interest group demands of the surrounding community (Selznick, 1949; Messinger, 1955; Gusfield, 1955; King, 1956; Sills, 1957; Clark, 1960; Zald and Ash, 1966; Demerath and Theissen, 1968; Cleveland et al., 1974). Although this body of literature has added greatly to our understanding of organizational behavior, the organizations studied by these researchers have been primarily characterized by a centralized authority structure. This leaves open the question of whether or not decentralized organizations adapt in the same way as centralized organizations (Litwak, 1970: 126-137; Brouillette and Quarantelli, 1971: 41).

In this chapter we shall examine what happened to NIN's behavior as a decentralized formal organization when it was threatened with a substantial loss of funding. Blau (1970: 151) has shown where the formalization of organizational procedures and centralization of authority do not necessarily occur simultaneously. NIN was one such formalized but decentralized organization which, in the fall of 1972, was temporarily caught in the squeeze for federal support. When the loss of funding seemed to be a certainty, a series of meetings was held by the organization in an effort to chart a plausible future. The results of these meetings are here recounted, accompanied by an examination of the impact of NIN's decentralized structure on the adaptation alternatives that were developed. Special attention is given to the analysis of three correlates of decentralization: (1) stress producing unstated goals, (2) a weak vertical and strong horizontal pattern of interactions within the hierarchy, and (3) a low level of membership commitment to the organization.

NIN expanded quite rapidly for the first two and one-half years of its existence. Toward the middle of the third year of its operations, the program had grown so much that a notable proportion of the participants in federal food stamp and food distribution programs were also receiving aid from NIN. When NIN had reached a peak of operations between January and April of 1972, a study commissioned by the United States Department of Agriculture (Control System Research, 1972) indicated that there existed a tremendous overlap in welfare services provided by the federal programs and NIN.

This report may be seen, in retrospect, as marking the initiation of a period during which the federal funds granted NIN were carefully scrutinized. In brief, arguments were made on the basis of this study that the needs of the citizenry could be effectively met by the existing federal programs and hence, there was no basis for continuing to fund NIN with federal money. It must be noted that, by this time, NIN was a large organization covering sixteen counties in the state of Washington. With a scope of operations this vast, NIN was forced to depend heavily on federal grants, and the prospect of losing these funds required a reassessment with respect to the future activity of the organization. Existing resources assured NIN's operation until summer of 1973, at which time the organization would have to readapt to its environment if no additional funds could be found.

Contrary to what one would predict from the literature on organizations faced with decline, such strategies as shifts to new goals, extensive modification of existing goals, and the prospect of closing down were not entertained as feasible options. Rather, the emergent pattern might be best described as the maintenance of existing goals on a localized and smaller scale. The remainder of this paper is devoted to the examination of the factors contributing to the organizational choice of continued goal maintenance as an adaptation to anticipated decline.

GOALS AND STRUCTURE

A recapitulation of NIN's early history is now desirable in order to clarify the specification of organizational goals and structure. The hunger problem stemming from high unemployment had been felt in Seattle for at least one year before NIN was conceived. During this period there existed a number of local, church affiliated food distribution centers which catered to people who, for one reason or another, did not qualify for aid under the federal programs. When meetings were initially held to develop a large-scale private helping agency, members of the church council of Greater Seattle, familiar with the success of the existing local centers, suggested that an organization which distributed food through local neighborhood food banks would be most effective in meeting the common goal: to feed the hungry.

Neighbors in Need was to consist of an administration with offices in Seattle and a number of neighborhood food banks. A director, an advisory council, warehouse personnel and a small research staff constituted the structure of the administration. The primary responsibilities of the administration involved coordinating the efforts of local food banks, drafting proposals for grants to expand or enhance services and to serve as liaison with the business sector and the community in general. The food banks were organized around a "coordinating volunteer" who reported to and received communications from the administration. Also, each food bank was to maintain enough additional volunteers to administer the business of the bank; that is, to distribute food and canvass the neighborhood for donations of food, volunteer support and cash. The major responsibilities of food banks, therefore, involved soliciting local donations and distributing food.

A crucial element in implementing the organization as outlined revolves around two issues. First, the funds available for getting the organization started were very limited. Second, the already functioning food distribution centers were readily convertible to "food banks" through the simple device of appointing a "coordinating volunteer"—complicated only by the problem of obtaining the consent of the center. Thus, the most plausible method of implementing NIN was to convince as many of the existing distribution centers as possible to convert to food banks and expend the funds necessary to establish "new" banks to cover neighborhoods where no distribution centers were operative. In terms of the general strategy of getting NIN on its feet, this tack was quite successful, but it had a major impact on the subsequent structure of internal relations in the organizations.

Eventually the bulk of NIN's food banks were converted distribution centers which joined the organization only after the sponsors were convinced that the centers would benefit from the alliance. In this way, the provision of services (coordination and message relay) and emergency support (food in the event of a local shortage) to the food banks became unstated goals (Catton, 1962). Furthermore, all food bank staff members were unpaid volunteers recruited from the local neighborhood. A major consequence of these conditions for NIN involved the development of a structural and physical separation of the administration from the food banks. This bifurcation of the organization was further complicated by the administration's implicit obligation to permit the food banks to maintain their autonomy and to provide inputs, in the form of services, to the banks. The impact of these structural conditions on patterns of commitment and flows of interaction within the organization may be seen as the major shaping factor in NIN's response to the threat of decline (Litwak and Hylton, 1962).

COMMITMENT AND INTERACTION

The effects of the administration-food bank separation are perhaps most evident when one examines membership commitment. Food bank volunteers constitute the bulk of the membership of NIN, and since they regularly labor long hours without pay, it may be assumed that they are committed to the organization's stated goal: feeding the hungry. It is important to emphasize, however, that members may be committed to the organizational goal and yet not to the organization (Zald and Denton, 1963).

Several conditions appear to reinforce the goal commitment of NIN's membership. Probably the most prominent among these is the fact that although the organization is large, member activities are more directly a part of organizational goal accomplishment than leader activities. Members of the organization distribute the goods, and experience the reinforcement of approaching goal achievement on a daily basis. In addition, the representatives of the administration are rarely present at food banks. The administration participates in food bank affairs only when asked and, even then, contact usually takes the form of a delivery from the warehouse. Thus members of the organization tend to characterize organizational officials as perfunctory support personnel to be summoned in emergencies only and not to be looked to as the guiding force in goal attainment.

This characterization of the officials as nonessential "helpers" is strengthened by the fact that most members of the organization were engaging in behavior oriented to feeding hungry people (NIN's major goal) long before the organization itself was established. It will be recalled that when NIN was founded, numerous existing food distribution centers "converted" to food banks. These distribution centers were built on personal relationships and staffed in some instances by people who were one time clients. While the number of new clients greatly increased as NIN received more publicity, this style of personal relationships was not destroyed. Indeed, old friendship ties between food distributors and clients persisted and new ties were formed. Administrators, being few in number, seldom seen at food banks, and having a mimimum of direct contact with food bank volunteers, could not, in response to stress, command any particular loyalty to the organization on the part of the membership (Barnekov and Rich, 1972: 735).

Finally, aside from the impact of regular, goal-related reinforcements which accrued to members and strong interpersonal ties, one must consider that the growth of member commitment to the organization was precluded to a large extent by the lack of a well-defined hierarchy of offices in NIN. In most voluntary associations, the election or appointment of a member to an office in the organization symbolizes, among other things, a reinforcement for the member, afforded him by the organization. To the extent that the bulk of member reinforcements flow from the organization, one expects commitment to the organization (Kunkel, 1970: 103-111). Most of the variety of reinforcements afforded the membership of NIN came from the work context of the food bank, while only a small number of reinforcements could be said to originate in the administration. Thus, the attachment to the organization which appears to accompany the "goal changing" or "goal modification" patterns of adaptation to decline is absent insofar as NIN is concerned.

The pattern of vertical and horizontal interactions within the organization may also be treated as a barometer of organizational cohesion (Guest, 1962: 82-105; Caplow, 1964: 256-258). Implicit in the preceding discussion is the idea that, in terms of the formal structure and sentiments within the organization, NIN may be seen as composed of two subgroups: the administration and the food banks (Selznick, 1948). Horizontal interactions both within administration and the food banks are predominant. The level of information flow, therefore, is high between food banks and within the administration, a condition suggesting that cohesion is high within each level of the organization (Simpson, 1959: 186).

In general, the level of vertical interaction is low relative to horizontal interaction. That is, communication and the flow of information between levels of the organization (administration and food banks) is kept at a minimum. The daily activity of the food banks centers on distribution, and since the banks depend on local donations and canvassing for the bulk of their operating supplies, there is little reason for them to initiate interactions with administration. The resultant low level of vertical interaction coupled with a comparatively high level of horizontal exchange may therefore be seen as a product of the previously mentioned structural bifurcation of NIN.

RESPONSE TO ENVIRONMENTAL STRESS

The preceding discussion of goal commitment, unstated goals, and patterns of internal interaction has served to make explicit several consequences of the structure of NIN. The procedures of NIN are formalized, and communication channels are established; but authority remains decentralized, offices are physically isolated, and the level of membership commitment to the organization *per se* is low. It is also to be emphasized that this combination of characteristics is not at all rare; indeed, the structure of many social movements and "grass roots" community organizations and action groups closely approximates the NIN condition (cf. Barth and Johnson, 1959; Wood, 1972; Thursz, 1972; Forrest, 1973). Given that this collection of structural characteristics is not unique, subsequent discussion focuses on the ways in which decentralization shapes organizational response to decline.

As it functioned in early 1973, NIN was a large and decentralized organization. Further, the structural bifurcation already described was reflected in the way the organization was funded. The food banks depended for the most part on their own activities (canvassing the neighborhood, etc.) for operating funds and appealed to the administration for additional funds or supplies in emergencies. On the other hand, the administration derived its operating capital from private donations and government grants (with the latter contributing most significantly) and was bound, by the previously mentioned unstated goals, to contribute to but not receive funds from the food banks. Hence, the impact of the loss of all federal grants to the organization had most immediate implications for the pattern of administrative funding. Also, it is clear that without regard to where the money was cut, the loss of federal grants required a scaling down of NIN's activity. This latter consequence is sufficient to define NIN as an organization faced with the problem of decline.

There are two general patterns of adaptation open to declining organizations. The pattern most often documented is structural centralization and consolidation, characterized by a trimming of the existing hierarchy, a general tightening of organizational objectives and the consolidation of existing resources. It was from the study of organizations opting for a centralization pattern that the concepts of "organizational modification," "co-optation," "coalition with existing organization" and "conversion to sustaining goals" were derived (cf. Selznick, 1949; Messinger, 1955; Zald and Ash, 1966). It has been noted, however, that neither of these concepts in particular nor the idea of centralization in general, were especially helpful in examining NIN, whose adaptation to decline involved a rather extreme decentralization. It is further suggested that organizations with structures similar to NIN foster leader-member relationships which preclude the possibility of an option to centralize and consolidate when faced with decline. In elaborating this claim, attention is turned to the leader-member interactions which preceded NIN's decision to continue small-scale operations if federal funds were lost.

When the leadership of NIN was first informed that the organization would lose its federal funding, several alternatives representing plausible courses of action were explored. Initially, it was suggested that the organization could sustain itself intact by locating different sources for funding. An intensive publicity campaign accompanied by private appeals to individuals who had previously made large contributions was launched, but netted donations which, compared to lost federal money, were small. It was judged that if done on a regular basis, such appeals would cost more than they would produce and, hence, such a strategy did not constitute a viable alternative to federal funding.

The second course of action suggested by the leadership, although protested by the membership, was consonant with what would be expected based on the existing organizational decline literature. The leaders were aware that in order to survive at all, a cutback in operations must be instituted. Thus, in keeping with what might be called "Michels' Hypothesis" (Michels, 1949), a modification of the primary goal, with tactical implications was proposed. It was argued that as far as changing the plight of the poor was concerned, the efforts of NIN could be best classified as a band-aid approach. The food banks only provided food to the hungry on a temporary basis without doing anything about the reasons for, or the causes of, that hunger. Political action (lobbying and drafting legislation) would be an effective way of instituting changes in the condition of the poor, but adopting it would entail ceasing administration services to the food banks, closing the warehouse, and for an "all-out" effort, closing the food banks and channeling the funds that they normally collected from canvassing into a lobbying fund. In essence, the administration's program involved abandoning the goal of directly feeding the hungry, consolidating the resources at hand, and adopting political tactics.

This second proposal developed by the administration predictably met with substantial protest from the membership. In suggesting that the goal of feeding the hungry be abandoned and the food banks be closed, the administration had blocked the major source of membership reinforcement. Since they received no salary and derived few rewards directly from the administration, there was little reason for the members to support the administration in what amounted to a very radical change in goals. Members suggested that the federal funding problem was the administration's difficulty and did not really affect the food banks. After all, most of the banks were still self-sufficient and could survive, as they did before, without the help of the administration.

This reaction on the part of the membership underscores the consequences of one crucial difference between the reactions of centralized and decentralized organizations to the prospect of decline. As Barth (1965) has noted, decentralization may involve a physical isolation of offices (in the present case, administration from members) and such separations serve as a major barrier to communication. With communications hampered, and the inability of administrators to mediate member reinforcement, control and consolidation in the face of environmental stress would be too much to expect from any leadership. For structural reasons, oligarchy and shifts in organizational goals become unreasonable.

Addressing the case in hand, NIN's membership opted to abandon the administration if all monies were lost and, instead, readjust the food banks to independent neighborhood operations. There was little overt conflict with administrative representatives over the decision; that is, the leadership was simply not defined as a force to be reckoned with. If NIN had not received a last minute refunding which insured an additional twelve months operation, the plan developed by the membership would have resulted in the disassembling of the administration and the total reorientation of food bank operations to the local neighborhood.

In reviewing NIN's response as a variation from the more frequently described patterns of centralized organizations, it is possible to focus on two major factors associated with centralization and note their relevance for NIN. It has been suggested that organization leaders play an important part in promoting centralization as an adaptation to decline. It is typically the leaders who initiate suggestions for consolidation and "sell" these ideas to the membership. Thus, a well-defined hierarchy of authority may be seen as a necessary factor in facilitating the development of centralization. NIN's administration could be called well defined, but it was not extensive and served more for coordination than command. The day-to-day operation of NIN involved the distribution of food, and this activity centered in the food banks. In addition, the administration did not participate directly in this activity, and decisions about the conduct of the distribution process were made at the food bank level. NIN, therefore, lacked certain structural prerequisites for centralization.

It bears mentioning also that, to successfully institute a change in goals, leaders must either convince the membership that the change is a very minor one, or rely on the member's attachment to the organization as a way of smoothing the transition from the old to the new (Gross, 1969). Put a different way, to effect the changes necessary to centralize a failing organization requires a high level of membership commitment to the organization. While spirits were high among members and there was considerable commitment to the goals, the commitment of NIN's membership to the organization *per se* was quite low.

In summary, this chapter has documented an infrequently reported variation of organizational response to environmental stress. The evidence assembled underscores the importance of the internal structure of the organization in addition to the nature of environmental conditions when predicting whether an organization will change or modify its goals as an adaptation to decline. It has been suggested that internal structure places certain restraints upon membership commitment to the organization which, in turn, has perhaps a greater impact on the character of an organization's transformation than the "style" or activities of the leadership. Most sociological studies of organizational decline have tended to emphasize only organization-environment relations, focusing primarily upon the organizational goals as put forth by the leaders and the support that these receive from the environment. The present study demonstrates the usefulness of taking into account the interplay between internal structure as well as the organization's relations with its environment. However, putting the theoretical implications of Chapters Three and Four aside, we find ourselves left without a discourse on the practical and applied considerations of this research effort on a community service organization. These issues, therefore, are the theme for Chapter Five.

5
Epilogue: Lessons Learned in Community Action

The foregoing account of the emergence and development of NIN has revealed a number of interwoven conditions which brought this organization into existence and facilitated its persistence. Having focused upon the theoretical question of interorganizational cooperation or competition, it remains to discuss the implications of the factors surrounding NIN's history, and to project some practical considerations for organizations which seek to service community needs.

Three general factors have emerged in this research as being particularly important with respect to the promotion of community welfare: (1) changing environmental conditions, (2) organizational adaptability, and (3) the nature of the goals pursued. Each of these dimensions may be seen to have bearing on the extent to which the organization is seen as legitimate in the community, and the extent to which it generates membership commitment within the organization. The achievement of legitimation and commitment, in turn, is crucial for the effective operation of any organization. In summarizing the applied aspects of the NIN research project, therefore, discussion will focus alternately on each of the above dimensions.

CHANGING ENVIRONMENTAL CONDITIONS

This study has documented an important organizational response to environmental change, in this case economic instability. In times of resource shortages, it would appear that organizations, indeed, do tend to shift from goal attainment strategies to survival maintenance. Although this might be quite appropriate for commodity producing organizations or even service organizations during periods of short-term instability, it seems only to compound a service organization's problems when there is a prolonged period of environmental instability. It is during such periods of economic deprivation that demands for community welfare are apt to increase. A gap is thus created between the level of community demands and the capacity of the existing organizations to fulfill these demands. This discrepancy between community needs and organizational service tends to undermine the legitimacy of the established system, and, concomitantly, generate a climate conducive to community innovation.

In Seattle, this climate fostered the emergence of NIN which, as has been shown, was designed by community action leaders for the purpose of filling the gap between community needs and organizational service. Indeed, organizational emergence is a major form of community adaptation which has been observed in a number of different stress situations (Quarantelli, 1970:2; Haas and Drabek, 1973:6-7; Forest, 1973). But is this manner of coping with resource shortage the most effective approach to be sponsored by a community?

Most of the literature on emergent organizations indicates that they come into being during periods of stress, perform as transitory interaction systems fulfilling unmet community tasks, and then dissolve after the emergency period has passed (Haas and Drabek, 1973: 6; Taylor et al., 1970: 79-108). But not all emergent organizations dissolve, as we have seen with NIN. The characterization of emergent organizations as short-lived may be due to the research on emergent organizations having focused primarily upon the sudden onset, short-duration impact distress situation, excluding for the most part the gradual onset, long-duration impact distress situations. Yet, as we have seen, the relative success in providing community service and the degree of member commitment displayed by a new organization depend in part on the length of the time lapse between the emergence of the organization and the initial response of existing organizations (Adler, 1965: 592-597). In addition, the specificity of the task orientation, the low degree of formality, and the high degree of face-to-face interaction indicates that persons who are involved in such organizations develop a commitment to the organization, irrespective of its effectiveness. Thus, it would seem that prolonged distress situations *per se* generate conditions which enhance the likelihood that organizations of this type will resist dissolution.

Viewing community actions in terms of a cost-benefit ratio, it would appear that unless the emergent organization is providing a service not already subsumed under the goals of the established system, then a modification of the established system in order to accommodate the changing environment would be more effective. Thompson and Hawkes (1962) have pointed out that alternative modes of adaptation to environmental instability include the established organizations (a) modifying their structure, (b) changing or extending their definition of the present task environment, and (c) developing "synthetic organizations" where there is a temporary alliance among existing organizations. Since this research has demonstrated, on the one hand, how established organizations tend to swing from goal attainment to survival maintenance (normative welfare organizations made qualifying for assistance more stringent, thereby insuring that funds would not be depleted by the excessive demand for aid) during periods of environmental distress and, on the other hand, how an emergent organization was successful in the short run, it may be possible to convince the leadership of established organizations that changes in the environment require corresponding changes in organizational structure and procedures. To illustrate, drawing upon the directed changes suggested by Thompson and Hawkes, several modes of adaptation may be advanced:

(1) *Structural modifications:* With all of its faults, a bureaucratic structure appears to be the most effective mode of organization during periods of environmental stability, but its standardized rules and procedures become blocks to effective goal attainment during times of environmental instability. It would seem that the decentralized structure and informal mode of operation, characteristic of NIN and other emergent organizations, appear to be a more effective means of implementing community service. There is no inherent reason why bureaucratic organizations, faced with environmental distress, could not put into effect an emergency decentralized mode of

organization. Officials could be relocated in strategic areas of need and given relative autonomy in decision making. The central office could be reduced to a skeleton crew, concerned principally with coordination. Paper work might be carried out on special short-form cards with only the information essential to task fulfillment recorded. These and other structural modifications, depending upon the nature of the distress, would seem necessary in order to break the mold which has traditionally made bureaucracy inept in the face of environmental change.

(2) *Redefining the task environment:* Bureaucracies typically pigeonhole their clients and standardize the service to be provided, but changes in the environment alter the composition and needs of persons requiring service. Standard classification schemes become inappropriate with changing conditions in the environment. Under conditions of environmental instability, bureaucratic leadership must increase their receptiveness to *community definitions* of need. A decentralized mobilization would facilitate feedback in this regard; however, careful attention would have to be given to an equitable distribution of service relative to organizational resources. In bypassing normal classification and procedural routing, methods would have to be devised for assessing the extent of need in various areas of the community. Again, the coordinating function, as opposed to an authoritarian function, would be manifest in an active bureaucratic adaptation to an unstable environment.

(3) *Organizational alliances:* During periods of environmental stress and increased community needs, cooperation among different organizations and community groups enhances the resource base for attacking problems, and also reduces the likelihood of providing overlapping services or depleting resources through competition. In order to promote a viable cooperation, bureaucratic leaders would have to temporarily overlook formal guidelines in recruiting personnel. In this way, organizations could effectively co-opt community manpower and volunteer service groups, using these to supplement their service to the community. By incorporating community action groups into the "bureaucratic" mobilization,

an organization would increase their effectiveness by gaining the addition of diverse and novel ways in providing service; for example, NIN's strategy of supplying bulk food. The action groups would also benefit by being able to draw upon the already established center of coordination. Resources spent on administration would therefore be minimized, while resources applied to problem solving would be maximized. Furthermore, since the "bureaucracy" would be coordinating the efforts, the commitment of involved persons would be likely to remain task centered and not become generalized to the organization itself. A return to normal conditions might thus entail member satisfaction with the problem's solution, rather than a frustrated and friction oriented seeking of organizational survival.

ORGANIZATIONAL ADAPTABILITY

It must be acknowledged that, with an established set of personnel to handle clients, the capacity of normative systems to adapt to change remains limited. There are several conditions which limit preparedness in a community's ability to adapt. To begin with, the various types and the actual amount of environmental change that occur can never be completely anticipated; environmental alterations can come from so many and varied agents, for example, floods, earthquakes, a failing economy, and the like. Their potential degree of impact is even more varied. This circumstance is exacerbated with the onset of progressive environmental distress, because the afflicted community constructs temporary, makeshift ideologies to reinforce the optimism of the collective regarding a solution to the situation's problem. The lack of response by existing welfare agencies and NIN's early faith in a government solution illustrate this point. In addition, Dynes (1970) illustrated that communities anticipate future environmental alterations in terms of past events and fail to prepare for the unexperienced. Finally, community preparedness also varies with happenstance factors: the season of the year and time of day. In Seattle, for example, it will be remembered that the job market was further tightened when the school system slowed operations during the summer months, releasing students into the community who were looking for temporary jobs.

Each of the above physical, social, and symbolic constraints upon the ability of a system to adapt to external change preserves the existence of particular unmet needs brought on by the increased demands being made upon the system. In general, the magnitude of environmental impact would seem to be inversely related to organizational adaptability. This means that external change of certain intensities or durations will create areas of unmet needs which cannot or will not be met instrumentally by the established normative system. The three overall modifications suggested in the discussion on environmental changes would seem also to provide possible correctives for these restraints on organizational adaptability. A decentralized structure, with an open receptivity to community feedback, and a working connection with other systems and groups would increase awareness of the change impacts, lessen dependence upon previous experience and, perhaps, allow better integration among various system outputs.

NATURE OF THE GOALS PURSUED

Emergent organizations come into being with clearly defined short-term objectives; for example, NIN sought to feed the unemployed. This is in contrast to bureaucracies which pursue more diffuse goals, such as sustaining community welfare. New organizations also contrast with established systems in that they are characterized by (1) loosely defined centers of power, (2) shortage of equipment and trained personnel, and (3) informal arrangement of their administrative structure. Each of these variables has been found to correlate positively with the short period of time that a new organization has been in existence (Tsouderos, 1955). Therefore, when the goals of new and established organizations overlap, and the established organizations are better equipped to achieve the goals, established systems should be expected to absorb the clientele of emergent organizations, leaving the new organization without an operating base. With a prolonged environmental impact, however, established organizations shift to survival maintenance, providing an opportunity for the new organization to become better organized and a potential competitor to the established organizations.

It has already been noted that the emergence of organizations is contingent upon the presence of certain conditions in the community social structure (Parr, 1970: 424-427; Lotz and Gillespie, 1972: 18-20); nevertheless, it can now be seen that a prolonged distress situation generates conditions which enhance the likelihood of competition. It is not argued that all new organizations under such conditions will compete, but that competition is an alternative to being absorbed by established organizations. Furthermore, new organizations are likely to resist being absorbed because their structure is less specialized or segmented, and they are serving a presumed community need which frequently leads to organizational solidarity and a desire to preserve the organization (cf. Tsouderos, 1955: 208-209).

These developments are quite understandable in terms of organizational outlooks, but from the standpoint of the community, it would appear to increase the cost of service and, hence, decrease the actual amount of service provided. This would seem to be the case only when an emergent organization pursues a goal that is already incorporated within an established system. The most efficient resolution again appears to be through convincing bureaucratic leaders of the need to increase their flexibility during periods of environmental alterations and community stress.

Notes

1. A number of ideas concerning emergent organizations and their persistence may be found in the collective behavior literature (Killian, 1962: 142; Smelser, 1963: 23; Turner, 1964: 382), but the approach here is to use data to inform our observations and thus develop rather than confirm hypotheses. See Forrest's (1973) study of a community welfare emergent organization for an example which draws upon the collective behavior literature.

2. Anderson and Dynes (1973: 330-341) have contributed an exception. Their research documents the May Movement in Curacao, an organization which was initiated by system stress based on the local economy.

3. An outstanding presentation of the relationship between output and support goals appears in Gross and Grambsch (1968: 7-9) or, for a fuller discussion, see Gross (1969).

4. This reveals an interesting theoretical discovery; that is, in order for domain consensus to result in cooperation, it must exist on all three of the variables comprising the domain consensus concept.

5. By "therapeutic community needs" Barton means that community members develop an increased awareness and concern for the welfare of other community members.

6. While this proposition seems to be tautological, it is not, because it refers to two different units of analysis: *organizational* tasks and *community* needs.

References

Adler, Franz

1965 "Hacia una sociologia del comportamiento creador." *Revista Mexicana de Sociologia* (Mayo-Agosto): 557-602.

Anderson, William A.

1969 *Local Civil Defense in Natural Disaster.* Columbus: Disaster Research Center, Ohio State University.

Anderson, William A., and Russell R. Dynes

1973 "Organizational and political transformation of a social movement: a study of the 30th of May movement in Curacao." *Social Forces* 51 (March): 330-341.

Barnekov, T., and D. Rich

1972 "The corporation as a social welfare institution." *American Behavioral Scientist* 15 (May): 749-764.

Barth, E. A. T.

1965 "Metropolitan decentralization through incorporation." *The Western Political Quarterly* 28 (March): 61-67.

Barth, E. A. T., and S. D. Johnson

1959 "Community power and a typology of social issues." *Social Forces* 28 (October): 29-32.

Barton, Allen

1969 *Communities in Disaster.* New York: Doubleday.

Blalock, Hubert H., Jr.

1969 *Theory Construction.* Englewood Cliffs: Prentice-Hall.

Blau, P.

1970 "Decentralization in bureaucracies," in Mayer Zald (ed.), *Power in Organizations.* Nashville: Vanderbilt University Press.

Blau, P. M., and M. W. Meyer

1971 *Bureaucracy in Modern Society.* Second Edition. New York: Random House.

Brouillette, John, and Enrico Quarantelli

1971 "Types of pattern variation in bureaucratic adaptions to organizational stress." *Sociological Inquiry* 41 (Winter): 39-46.

Buckley, William

1967 *Sociology and Modern Systems Theory.* New Jersey: Prentice-Hall.

Campbell, Donald T., and Julian C. Stanley

1963 *Experimental and Quasi-experimental Designs for Research.* Chicago: Rand McNally.

Cantril, Hadley

1941 *The Psychology of Social Movements.* New York: Wiley.

Caplow, T.

1964 *Principles of Organization.* New York: Harcourt, Brace and World.

Catton, W.

1962 "Unstated goals as a source of stress in an organization." *Pacific Sociological Review* 5 (Spring): 29-35.

Chapin, F., and J. Tsouderos

1956 "The formalization process in voluntary associations." *Social Forces* 30 (June): 342-345.

Clark, Burton R.

1960 *The Open-Door College.* New York: McGraw-Hill.

Cleveland, Charles, Ronald Perry, and David Gillespie

1974 "The contributions of conflict to social movement stabilization." *International Journal of Group Tensions* IV (December): 395-407.

Cohen, M. R., and E. Nagel

1934 *An Introduction to Logic and Scientific Method.* New York: Harcourt, Brace and World.

Control Systems Research

1972 Data Report for U.S. Department of Agriculture, contract number 12-35-600-77. Arlington, Virginia.

Congressional Record

1971 Day of 5 May. Washington, D. C.

1971 Day of 17 May. Washington, D. C.

Demerath, N. J., and Victor Theissen

1966 "On spitting against the wind: organizational precariousness and American irreligion." *American Journal of Sociology* (May): 674-687.

Dynes, Russell

1970 *Organized Behavior in Disaster.* Lexington, Massachusetts: D. C. Heath and Company.

Dynes, Russell, Eugene Haas, and Enrico Quarantelli

1967 "Administrative methodological, and theoretical problems of disaster research." *Indian Sociological Bulletin* 4 (June): 215-227.

Emery, F. E., and E. L. Trist
1972 "The causal texture of organizational environments," in Brinkerhoff and Kunz (eds.), *Complex Organizations and Their Environments.* Dubuque, Iowa: William C. Brown Company.

Evan, William M.
1972 "The organizational set: toward a theory of interorganizational relations," pp. 326-340, in Merlin B. Brinkerhoff and Philip R. Kunz (eds.), *Complex Organizations and Their Environments.* Dubuque, Iowa: William C. Brown Company.

Festinger, Leon, Henry W. Riecken, and Stanley Schachter
1953 *When Prophecy Fails.* New York: Harper Torchbooks.

Forest, Thomas R.
1973 "Needs and group emergence." *American Behavioral Scientist* 16 (February): 413-425.

Gillespie, David, and Ronald W. Perry
1974 "Metascientific considerations in the community power controversy." *Research Studies* 42: 123-127.

Gross, Edward
1969 "The definition of organizational goals." *British Journal of Sociology* XX (September): 277-294.

Gross, Edward, and Paul V. Gramsch
1968 *University Goals and Academic Power.* Washington, D. C.: American Council on Education.
1974 *Changes in University Organization, 1964-1971.* New York: McGraw Hill.

Guest, R.
1962 *Organizational Change.* Illinois: Irwin-Dorsey.

Gusfield, Joseph R.
1955 "Social structure and moral reform: a study of the woman's christian temperance union." *American Journal of Sociology* 61 (November): 221-232.

Haas, Eugene, and Thomas Drabek
1973 *Complex Organizations: A Sociological Perspective.* New York: Macmillan.

Hage, Jerald, and Michael Aiken
1969 "Routine technology, social structure, and organizational goals." *Administrative Science Quarterly* 14 (September): 366-377.

Hall, Richard H.
1972 *Organizations: Structure and Process.* Englewood Cliffs: Prentice-Hall.

Johnson, Bryan
1971 "Seattle Northwest Feature." Broadcast on KOMO Radio, December 10, 1971. Seattle, Washington.

Katz, Daniel, and Robert L. Kahn
1972 "Organizations and the system concept," in Brinkerhoff and Kunz (eds.), *Complex Organizations and Their Environments.* Dubuque, Iowa: William C. Brown Company.

Killian, Lewis
1962 "Leadership in the desegregation crisis," in M. Sherif (ed.), *Intergroup Relations and Leadership.* New York: Wiley.

King, C.
1956 *Social Movements in the United States.* New York: Random House.

Klapp, Orrin
1969 *Collective Search for Identity.* New York: Holt, Rinehart and Winston.

Kunkel, J.
1970 *Society and Economic Growth.* New York: Oxford University Press.

Lawrence, Paul, and Jay Lorsch
1967 *Organizations and Environment.* Boston: Harvard University Press.

Levine, Sol, and Paul E. White
1961 "Exchange as a conceptual framework for the study of interorganizational relationships." *Administrative Science Quarterly* 5 (March): 583-601. Citations are drawn from a reprint of this article in Brinkerhoff and Kunz (eds.), *Complex Organizations and Their Environments.* Dubuque, Iowa: William C. Brown Company, 1972.

Lipset, Seymour, Martin Trow, and James Coleman
1956 *Union Democracy.* Glencoe, Illinois: Free Press.

Litwak, E.
1970 "An approach to linkage in 'grass roots' community organization," in F. Cox et al. (eds.), *Strategies of Community Organization.* Itasca: Peacock.

Litwak, Eugene, and Lydia F. Hylton
1962 "Interorganizational analysis: a hypothesis on co-ordinating agencies." *Administrative Science Quarterly* 6 (March): 395-420.

Lotz, Roy, and David F. Gillespie
1972 "Isomorphic attraction: an a priori approach to social

movement participation." *Western Sociological Review* III (June): 14-26.

Magnuson, Warren
1971 Speech delivered on floor of United States Senate, December 9, 1971, Washington, D. C.

Messinger, Sheldon
1955 "Organizational transformation: a case study of a declining social movement." *American Sociological Review* 20 (February): 3-10.

Michels, R.
1949 *Political Parties*. Illinois: The Free Press.

Mileti, Dennis S.
1975 *Disaster Relief and Rehabilitation in the United States*. Boulder, Colorado: Institute of Behavioral Science, University of Colorado, Monograph # NSF-RA-E-75-009.

Mileti, Dennis S., and David F. Gillespie
1976 "An integrated formalization of organization-environment interdependencies." *Human Relations* 29 (January): 85-100.

Mileti, Dennis S., Thomas E. Drabek, and J. Eugene Haas
1975 *Human Systems in Extreme Environments: A Sociological Perspective*. Boulder, Colorado: Institute of Behavioral Science, University of Colorado, Monograph # NSF-RA-E-75-013.

Palumbo, Dennis J.
1969 "Power and role specificity in organization theory." *Public Administration Review* 29 (May-June): 237-248.

Parr, Arnold
1970 "Organizational response to community crises and group emergence." *American Behavioral Scientist* (March): 420-433.

Price, J. L.
1960 "Design of proof in organizational research." *Administrative Science Quarterly* 5: 121-134.

Quarantelli, Enrico L.
1970 "Emergent accommodation groups: beyond current collective behavior typologies." Reprint #51 from the Disaster Research Center, Ohio State University. This article also appears in *Human Nature and Collective Behavior: Papers in Honor of Herbert Blumer*, ed. Tamotsu Shibutani. Englewood Cliffs, New Jersey: Prentice-Hall, pp. 111-123.

Rushing, William A.

1968 "Hardness of material as related to division of labor in manufacturing industries." *Administrative Science Quarterly* 13 (September): 229-245.

Ruppert, Ray

1971 "Religion Section." *The Seattle Times,* Wednesday, August 18, 1971. Seattle, Washington.

Schrag, C.

1967 "Elements of theoretical analysis in sociology," in L. Gross (ed.), *Sociological Theory: Inquiries and Paradigms,* pp. 220-253. New York: Harper and Row.

Select Committee on Nutrition and Human Needs

1971 "Seattle: unemployment, the poor, and hunger." Washington, D. C.: United States Senate Special Report.

Selltiz, C., M. Jahoda, M. Deutsch, and S. W. Cook

1959 *Research Methods in Social Relations.* New York: Holt, Rinehart and Winston.

Selznick, Philip

1949 *TVA and the Grass Roots.* Berkeley: University of California Press.

1948 "Foundations of the Theory of Organizations," *American Sociological Review* 13: 25-35.

Sills, David L.

1957 *The Volunteers: Means and Ends in a National Organization.* Glencoe, Illinois: Free Press.

Sjoberg, Gideon, and Roger Nett

1968 *A Methodology for Social Research.* New York: Harper and Row.

Smelser, Neal

1963 *A Theory of Collective Behavior.* New York: Free Press.

Starbuck, William H.

1965 "Organizational Growth and Development," in J. G. March (ed.), *Handbook of Organizations,* pp. 451-533. Chicago: Rand McNally.

Stinchcombe, Arthur L.

1965 "Social structure and organizations," in James G. March (ed.), *Handbook of Organizations,* pp. 142-193. Chicago: Rand McNally.

Taylor, James B., Louis A. Urcher, and William H. Key

1970 *Tornado.* Seattle: University of Washington Press.

Taylor, Patricia

1971 *Neighbors in Need: Phase I.* Unpublished organizational literature.

Terreberry, Shirley
1968 "The evolution of organizational environments." *Administrative Science Quarterly* (March): 590-613.

Thompson, James, and Robert Hawkes
1962 "Disaster, community organization and administrative process," in *Man and Society in Disaster,* George Baker and Dwight Chapman (eds.) New York: Basic Books.

Thursz, R.
1972 "Community participation." *American Behavioral Scientist* 15 (May-June): 733-748.

Tsouderos, John E.
1955 "Organizational change in terms of a series of selected variables." *American Sociological Review* 20 (April): 206-210.

Turner, Ralph
1964 "Collective behavior," in R. E. L. Faris (ed.), *Handbook of Modern Sociology.* Chicago: Rand McNally.

Whetten, David A.
1975 "A general contingency approach to the design of interorganizational service delivery systems." Faculty Working Paper #286, College of Commerce and Business Administration: University of Illinois at Urbana - Champaign.

Williams, Steven R.
1971 *First year data report: nin.* Unpublished organizational literature.

Wood, J.
1972 "Unanticipated consequences of organizational coalitions." *Social Forces* 50 (June): 512-521.

Woodward, Joan
1965 *Industrial organization: theory and practice.* Oxford, England: Oxford University Press.

Zald, M., and R. Ash
1966 "Social movement organizations: growth, decay, and change." *Social Forces* (June): 327-340.

Zald, Mayer N., and Patricia Denton
1963 "From evangelism to general service: the transformation of the YMCA." *Administrative Science Quarterly* 8 (September): 214-234.

Zelditch, Morris, Jr.
1962 "Some methodological problems of field studies." *American Sociological Review* 67 (March): 566-576.

CARI
Comparative Administration Research Institute

Government, business, industrial, and educational organizations of every description have become more and more involved in international activities. The rapid acceleration of this involvement has been accompanied by a growing awareness of the intercultural aspects of administration. Thus, considerable research activity has been directed toward the cross-cultural study of organizations, resulting in a corresponding expansion of the literature. These developments stimulated the founding of CARI, the Comparative Administration Research Institute, within the Graduate School of Business at Kent State University. CARI was formed with these objectives:

to provide orientation and concentration for scholars interested and actively engaged in comparative administration;

to promote and direct specific research projects;

to establish and maintain contacts with individual scholars and research organizations;

to publish and disseminate research findings.

CARI's focus is on the field of administration, conceived to be a universal phenomenon of formalized group activity. Specific emphasis is placed on the integration and unification of organizational administration knowledge from the comparative, theoretical, and empirical approaches. However, broad dimensions also are pursued in intercultural, interinstitutional, international, and interdisciplinary studies.

The Institute has adopted a many-faceted approach to meet its objectives. It conducts annually a conference on specific topics of current research interest in the organization and administration areas. The conference attracts distinguished scholars from the United States, Canada, Europe, and elsewhere who present findings of their pioneering research.

In order to disseminate research findings, the Institute publishes a quarterly journal: *Organization and Administrative Sciences.* A distinctive feature of the journal is that it concentrates occasionally on full-length studies on a given issue. The Institute also publishes monographs and books on topics that are considered to be vital for the development of organizational and administrative knowledge. A partial listing of CARI publications follows.

C A R I Publications

Organizational Effectiveness, Lee Spray (ed.), 1976

Leadership Frontiers, James Hunt and Lars Larson (eds.), 1975

General Systems and Organization Theory: The Methodological Aspects, Arlyn Melcher (ed.), 1976

Group Decision Making and Effectiveness, Andrew Van de Ven, 1974

The Manager and The Man, George England, O. Dhingra, and Naresh Agarwal (eds.), 1974

Organization Theory and Interorganizational Analysis, Anant Negandhi, 1973

Human Resources: Manpower Policy and Planning Approaches, Elmer Burrack and Thomas McNichols, 1973

Conflict and Power in Complex Organizations: An Inter-Institutional Perspective, Anant Negandhi (ed.), 1972 (out of print)

Organization Theory in an Interorganizational Perspective, Anant Negandhi (ed.), 1971

Environmental Settings in Organizational Functioning, Anant Negandhi (ed.), 1970

Organizational Behavior Models, Anant Negandhi and Joseph Schwitter (eds.), 1970 (out of print)

Comparative Administration Management Conference Proceedings, 1968, Anant Negandhi, Arlyn Melcher, Joseph Schwitter (eds.), 1968 (out of print)

Forthcoming:

Management of Work: A Socio-Technical Systems Approach Thomas Cummings and Suresh Srivastva

Organization and Administrative Sciences

This Journal is published quarterly by the Comparative Administration Research Institute (CARI), a research unit in the Graduate School of Business Administration at Kent State University. It is an international publication devoted to research in organization theory and cross-cultural comparative studies.

One of the distinct features of *Organization and Administrative Sciences* is the occasional publication of a full-length, intensive, single study in a given issue. These studies are theoretical and empirical in nature and represent a significant contribution to the literature.

Some Representative Articles and Authors Appearing In Recent Past Issues:

"An Adaptive-Reactive Theory of Leadership: The Role of Macro Variables In Leadership Research," Richard N. Osborn and James G. Hunt, Summer-Fall 1975.

"A Systems Model of Societal Regulation," Walter Buckley, Spring, 1975.

"Culture and Organizational Systems," William M. Evan, Winter 1974/1975.

"Self-Management and Participation: Two Concepts of Democratization in Organizations," Cornelis J. Lammers, Winter 1974/1975.

"Some Unanswered Questions on Organizational Conflict," V. V. Murray, Winter 1974/1975.

"External Affairs: A Corporate Function in Search of Conceptualization and Theory," Jean Boddewyn, Spring 1974.

"The Institutional Function in Organization Theory," Talcott Parsons, Spring 1974.

A journal devoted to research in organization theory and behavior. Quarterly. $15 annual subscription.

The Kent State University Press Kent, Ohio 44242